kids' rooms
DESIGNS FOR LIVING

Meredith®
BOOKS

KIDS' ROOMS DESIGNS FOR LIVING®

Editor: Paula Marshall
Contributing Editor: Catherine M. Staub, Lexicon
    Consulting, Inc.
Contributing Associate Editor and Writer: Julie Collins,
    Lexicon Consulting, Inc.
Contributing Assistants: Bridget Nelson, Holly Reynolds,
    Megan Stotmeister, Lexicon Consulting, Inc.
Graphic Designer: On-Purpos, Inc.
Copy Chief: Terri Fredrickson
Publishing Operations Manager: Karen Schirm
Senior Editor, Asset and Information Manager: Phillip Morgan
Edit and Design Coordinator: Mary Lee Gavin
Editorial and Design Assistant: Renee E. McAtee
Book Production Managers: Pam Kvitne, Marjorie J.
    Schenkelberg, Rick von Holdt, Mark Weaver
Contributing Copy Editor: Jane Woychick
Contributing Proofreaders: Sue Fetters, Heidi Johnson,
    Vivian Mason
Contributing Indexer: Stephanie Reymann, Indexing
    Solutions

Meredith® Books

Executive Director, Editorial: Gregory H. Kayko
Executive Director, Design: Matt Strelecki
Managing Editor: Amy Tincher-Durik
Executive Editor/Group Manager: Benjamin W. Allen
Senior Associate Design Director: Tom Wegner
Marketing Product Manager: Brent Wiersma
National Marketing Manager—Home Depot: Suzy Emmack

Publisher and Editor in Chief: James D. Blume
Editorial Director: Linda Raglan Cunningham
Executive Director, New Business Development: Todd M. Davis
Director, Sales—Home Depot: Robb Morris
Executive Director, Sales: Ken Zagor
Director, Operations: George A. Susral
Director, Production: Douglas M. Johnston
Director, Marketing: Amy Nichols
Business Director: Jim Leonard

Vice President and General Manager: Douglas J. Guendel

Meredith Publishing Group

President: Jack Griffin
Executive Vice President: Karla Jeffries

Meredith Corporation

Chairman of the Board: William T. Kerr
President and Chief Executive Officer: Stephen M. Lacy

In Memoriam: E.T. Meredith III (1933–2003)

The Home Depot®

Marketing Manager: Tom Sattler

Distributed by Meredith Corporation.
Meredith Corporation is not affiliated with The Home Depot®.

Note to the Reader: Due to differing conditions, tools and individual skills, Meredith Corporation and The Home Depot® assume no responsibility for any damages, injuries suffered, or losses incurred as a result of attempting to replicate any of the home improvement ideas portrayed or otherwise following any of the information published in this book. Before beginning any project, including any home improvement project, review the instructions carefully and thoroughly to ensure that you or your contractor, if applicable, can properly complete the project, and, if any doubts or questions remain, consult local experts or authorities. Because codes and regulations vary greatly, you should always check with authorities to ensure that your project complies with all applicable local codes and regulations. Always read and observe all of the safety precautions provided by any tool or equipment manufacturer and follow all accepted safety procedures.

We are dedicated to providing inspiring, accurate and helpful do-it-yourself information. We welcome your comments about improving this book and ideas for other books we might offer to home improvement enthusiasts.
Contact us by any of these methods:
Leave a voice message at: 800/678-2093
Write to:
    Meredith Books, Home Depot Books
    1716 Locust St.
    Des Moines, IA 50309-3023
Send e-mail to: hi123@mdp.com

contents

how to use this book

Creating a room that captures the interests and personality of your children ensures they will have a personalized place for all activities from playtime during the day to sweet dreams at night. Before the decorating fun begins, the first step in designing any child's room involves determining the materials, colors, and style that fit that child best.

That's why the designers and associates at The Home Depot® have put together a collection of attractive, functional, and fun kids' rooms in one easy-to-use book. *Kids' Rooms Designs for Living* will inspire you with hundreds of photos and ideas on how to create an ideal room that fits your child and his or her tastes.

Whether you intend to design all or part of the room yourself or plan to use the services of an interior designer, you'll need a resource for ideas and some good advice on the latest trends and safety considerations for kids' room designs. That's where this book comes in.

STYLE-FUNCTION-DETAILS

Like any other room in the house, a child's bedroom, playroom, or bathroom deserves a design that combines style, function, and details. Good design is the result of defining your child's personal style and taste (or your own if your child is very young), considering how your children will use the space now and in the future, and remembering the fine elements that will make the space complete.

Style. The style of your child's room is a top priority. A decorating scheme can begin with a specific color, pattern, or theme. With the style in place, decisions about specific furnishings and materials will be easier. The time and effort you put into this phase will determine how happy you and your child will be with the finished room.

Function. Style is important, but the components of your child's room must be functional too. Consider furnishings and storage options and how they can aid the function and accessibility of your child's space. Design for the age your child is now while keeping in mind that kids grow quickly and need a space that can adapt to their future needs.

Details. To design a fully decorated room that beckons your child day after day, pay attention to the elements that complete the space, including lighting, window treatments, fabrics, and decorative objects.

nurseries

Welcome your little one home to a well-designed sleeping space that includes all the necessities—and a dose of style to boot. Whether you're decorating for a boy or a girl, combine the basic furnishings—including a crib, changing table, and comfortable chair—with a scheme that's right for you and your bundle of joy. Whimsical? Playful? Classic? It's up to you.

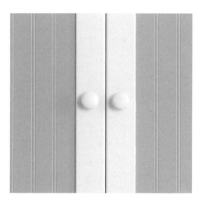 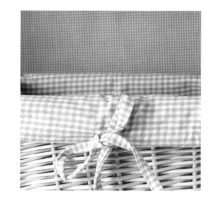 

BALANCING ACT
The white bedding and striped bedskirt on the circular crib act as a counterpoint to the plethora of polka dots in this room.

SOLID IDEA (ABOVE) White furnishings and accessories paired with a solid-color rocking chair and ottoman provide gender-neutral decor in this reading corner.

playful in polka dots

COLOR AND COMFORT. Even if the gender of your baby is unknown, it's still possible to create a nursery that's ready for his or her arrival. The polka-dot fabric used on the window treatments in this gender-neutral nursery inspired the playful design scheme, while stripes, flower-pattern pillows, and animal-shape artwork keep things interesting.

More important than the decor, however, is the quality of mattress you choose for the crib. A foam mattress is an inexpensive, durable option, although firm innerspring mattresses with a minimum of 150 coils often maintain their shape better.

gender-neutral decorating

Are you having a boy or a girl? Not sure? No problem.

Your child's nursery can still make a statement even if the sex of the baby is a secret. The key is to move beyond the standard little-girl pink and baby-boy blue color schemes. Go with playful yellow and serene green, khaki with red, or even the multitude of bold hues featured in the nursery at right.

Themes are a possibility too. Select a theme that appeals to *you;* chances are your child will want something different in a few years anyway. Consider basing a decorating scheme on an enjoyable activity, antique toys, or a favorite storybook character.

If you still want a few feminine or masculine touches in your child's space, get the basics (such as warm woodtone furnishings or neutral-color wall paint) in place; then add the gender-specific details after your little one is born.

GO DOTTY (BELOW) The frame of the mirror above the crib incorporates the circle motif inspired by the curtains.

COLORFUL IDEA (ABOVE) Painting the cabinet inserts of this wardrobe orange adds visual variety that fits the color scheme.

BIG BED Although babies spend their first few years sleeping in a crib, this room is large enough to fit a daybed as well, which ensures the space is comfortable for grown-ups spending time in the nursery.

EASY TREATMENT (LEFT) A wood cornice installed over the nursery window is painted with the same periwinkle stripes as the walls. The shade blocks light while baby sleeps.

the right stripes

NEW HEIGHTS. Soft hues can be soothing without being a snooze. In this room solid periwinkle blue paint covers the wall below the chair rail, while lighter periwinkle and white stripes stretch above to create the appearance of height under the sloped ceiling.

The result is a color scheme that's bright enough to be cheerful and strong enough to pull together the mix of new and used white-painted furniture. For history and visual interest, additional elements include an old green trunk, vintage quilts and bedspreads, and pages from an antique children's book that are framed above the crib for instant art.

BUMPERS FOR BABY. Many bedding sets include crib bumper pads. Besides adding a decorative element to the crib, the pads are supposed to prevent children from sticking their arms and legs through the crib slats or hitting their heads. Many children's safety organizations suggest that these pads be removed from the crib because they pose the risk of suffocation. If you choose to use bumpers, make certain they are thin, flat, and firmly secured to the crib at the corners, top, and bottom of the pads.

CREATIVE DISPLAY (LEFT) An existing nook enhanced with painted-to-match shutters provides display space for books and toys.

MADE FOR BABY (LEFT) Blue and white baby clothing becomes part of the decor when hung from pegs on the wall.

SIMPLE BACKDROP
(LEFT) Wallpaper in a hue
that matches the painted
walls provides a backdrop
for the white bookshelf,
which displays classic
children's books and
fabric-lined baskets.

SUPER STRIPES (ABOVE) Vertical
stripes add height to an attic room.
A white chair rail pairs with solid-
color periwinkle paint to create the
impression of wainscoting on the
lower half of the wall.

ENCHANTED FLOOR PLAN (ABOVE) All of the furnishings in this fairy-tale room line the wall, providing plenty of space for children to play on the floor. Wall murals further distinguish different areas.

COZY CORNER

(ABOVE) A tree painted on the wall towers over a reading corner filled with comfortable pillows. The shelf on the wall is low enough for little ones to reach books.

magic kingdom

ONCE UPON A TIME. When a toddler boy bunks with his baby brother, the room design must rise to the occasion. The Prince Rowan painting above the bed—a fitting piece of art for a toddler of the same name—inspired the fairy-tale room, which includes fanciful wall murals of a castle (shown on page 16) and a towering tree. Simple furnishings—including a crib and changing table for the baby and a bed and dresser for big brother—ensure the room is as functional for both boys as it is fun.

FAIRY-TALE DETAILS. In the company of colorful walls and bedding, the windows are bare of decoration aside from shades that block the light. A leaf suspended above the bed adds a playful touch, as do castle-theme draperies covering the closet doors (see page 17).

ARTISTIC FINISH
(RIGHT) Stencils and freehand skills were used to create the murals on the wall. Done in acrylic paint, this artwork can easily be painted over when it's time for a new theme.

BABY TIME (BELOW) A Prince Brayden sign hangs in the baby's corner, which includes a laundry hamper and changing table with wicker-basket storage. The castle mural above the table occupies the baby's attention at changing time.

nursery
checklist

Every nursery requires a crib and changing table. Beyond the basics, consider:

▸ **BEDDING.** The best fabrics for a baby crib are tightly woven cotton or a cotton and polyester blend. Keep bedding to a minimum, however, as it poses a safety hazard. (See page 35 for more information on bedroom safety precautions.)

▸ **FURNISHINGS.** If space is available include a chair for rocking baby. Purchase additional clothing storage such as a dresser or armoire that can grow with your child. Add toy boxes and bookshelves to corral all the belongings your baby is bound to accumulate.

▸ **WINDOW TREATMENTS.** Newborns may sleep at any time, day or night, so select window treatments that fully block out light. Consider safety here too: Keep curtains and cords out of your baby's reach.

PERSONAL SPACE (ABOVE) When siblings share a room, it's important that each child have a separate spot for storing belongings. A black-painted dresser located next to the toddler's bed holds his clothing and stores toys in easy-to-reach wicker baskets.

a kick of color

THOUGHTFUL CHOICES. The right color choices ensure longer life for your design scheme. With turquoise instead of baby blue and bold magenta instead of pale pink, this nursery can easily transition into an older child's room. Although this version of the room was made for a little girl, it would be easy to change if the new arrival turns out to be a boy: Swap the pink items for the cinnamon-watermelon red in the striped cushions.

SIDS SAFETY. Selecting color and furnishings for a baby's room can be fun. However, there's also a serious side to outfitting a nursery. Each year in the United States, approximately 2,500 children under one year old die from sudden infant death syndrome (SIDS). To reduce the risk of SIDS, babies should always sleep on their backs on a firm, flat mattress. Remove blankets, quilts, pillows, stuffed toys, and other soft items from the crib before sleep. Loose blankets are dangerous for babies, so use a wearable blanket or sleeper for warmth instead if needed.

TIME TO RENEW
(BELOW) A vintage dresser receives a jolt of color without losing its charm, thanks to a coat of durable magenta semigloss paint.

NEW VIEW (BELOW) This fully functional dresser doubles as a changing table. The slim mirror below the top shelf will occupy baby during diaper changing.

ARTFUL ENDEAVOR (BELOW)
Artwork can be affordable if you get creative. This grouping was created by appliquéing fabric shapes to squares of fabric stretched over artist's canvas.

delicious contrast

BROWN & BLUE ALL OVER. Get creative in a new nursery by moving beyond standard color schemes and paint treatments. This sophisticated little boy's nursery is a study in creating a yummy, modern color scheme made to last. A wall painted with random-width stripes of pale blue, chocolate, mocha, and cream sets the scene for the room. Brown is a warm, neutral color that works in almost any room; pairing chocolate with cool blue works so well because they are complementary colors. To really make the brown and blue details pop, the dresser and crib were painted cream to match the color of the rocker and ottoman. Polka dots on the bedding, window treatment fabrics, and bathroom walls (shown on page 23) provide a welcome contrast from the bold stripes.

IN CIRCLES (RIGHT) Round cribs provide a distinctive focal point for a baby's room. They often take up more space than a standard rectangular crib, so careful measurements are a must.

GO BROWN (LEFT) Brown paint on the cream-color dresser drawers adds a subtle accent that matches the brown piping on a nearby upholstered chair and ottoman.

GO DOTTY Blinds and polka-dot curtains with blackout linings ensure this nursery is dark enough for naps or early bedtimes. The throw pillow on the chair is the reverse of the curtain pattern.

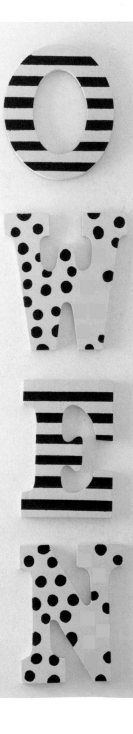

NEXT DOOR (LEFT)
Rather than duplicating
the bedroom stripes, the
bathroom walls feature
white bubbles. Having
a bathroom nearby will
be convenient when the
child is old enough to
bathe on his own.

color vision

An adult's vision may be 40 times better than a newborn's, but babies' vision improves quickly.

Some of the first colors babies see are reds, greens, and yellows, but they have trouble distinguishing between similar shades. By two months a baby can perceive subtle shadings, and by around eight months he or she can see as well as you. While it may seem a baby prefers a certain color, it's likely he or she is attracted to the brightness, darkness, or contrast of an object against its surroundings rather than the specific color. High-contrast edges and patterns are visually appealing to newborns, which makes black and white patterns a good choice. Encouraging interest in primary colors may help stimulate your child, but if primary colors aren't appealing, choose colors *you* like now—soon your little one will have his or her own color tastes.

NAME TAG (RIGHT)
Decorative details,
such as these blue-
painted wooden letters
adorned with stripes
and spots, further the
color scheme.

CHANGING STATION
(LEFT) A helpful
elephant corrals diapers
near the changing
table, which flips over
to become a chest
of drawers once baby
is grown.

jungle pals

GENTLE CREATURES. This jungle-theme nursery is a safe, soothing sanctuary for a little one. The furnishings and materials were chosen because they can grow with the child, plus they're made for snuggle time. The numerous comforting surfaces include an overstuffed rocker and ottoman, a fleece-covered bench cushion, and a soft cotton rag rug in the center of the room.

The highlight of this sweet, gender-neutral room is the artwork. Cuddly animals from a wallpaper border were turned into custom artwork displayed above the seating area (shown on pages 26–27). And the soft creatures that gaze down at the crib are 3-D animal babies created by a seamstress and attached to oversize panels.

WOOD UNDERFOOT. Newborns spend a lot of time in their parents' arms, but in no time they'll be crawling on the floor. Look for flooring materials that are kid-friendly and easy to clean. Wood flooring is an attractive choice, and it traps fewer allergens than carpet, which is a boon if family members suffer from allergies. Make certain little ones are comfortable on the floor by adding a soft area rug. Back the rug with nonskid material to keep it in place and to prevent slips.

SOFT SPOT (LEFT)
The cushion on the
movable window seat
is upholstered in fleece.
Storage bins underneath
are low enough to be
accessible when baby
becomes a toddler.

COLORFUL FRIENDS Friendly animals occupy the wall above the crib. Deeper tones of the ribbon stripes on the cafe curtains kick the zippy color palette up another notch.

VERSATILE ITEM

(LEFT) A small bookcase holds toys and books. Because of its simple cottage style, the bookcase can be moved to a family room or guest room later.

SNEAKY STORAGE (ABOVE) Extra blankets or pajamas are close at hand in this convenient undercrib drawer.

FLOOR PLANNING (BELOW) Measuring the nursery and planning furniture placement before buying pieces ensures that the furnishings will fit, particularly if space is tight.

EASY TO CLEAN
This cushy rocker
banishes any worries
about spills. The
white slipcover can be
removed in a snap
for washing.

under the big top

A FAIR ADAPTATION. Sometimes an over-the-top nursery theme is exactly what parents want. At other times a theme with nostalgic and subtle roots is a better fit. This nursery perfectly executes the latter with warm, understated style. A novelty-print fabric depicting circus vignettes on a tea-stained background inspired the concept for the room. Cream-stripe wallpaper extends below a chair rail, and the cream-dot wallpaper above stretches to the ceiling. Handpainted circus scenes on the crib's headboard and coordinating toy box and footstool continue the theme.

A STUDY IN BALANCE. Using complementary fabrics with the same color proportions as the main print in the decorating scheme provides balance and continuity. Here coordinating checks, stripes, prints, and solids round out the performance.

MERRY-GO-ROUND

(LEFT) Festive fair scenes were handpainted on the ends of the crib. Similar scenes adorn the nearby toy box.

CUDDLING CORNER A handpainted wallhanging emblazoned with the baby's name repeats the pennant motif of the window cornice and keeps watch over a green gingham-check rocking chair and footstool.

NOVELTY PRINT

(RIGHT) Pennants made from the signature print are layered on the bolstered cornice that adorns the window.

LOOKING UP (BELOW) The subtle alternating stripes of color on the ceiling slope toward the chandelier in the center of the room to create the feel of a circus tent.

bassinet or crib

A bassinet is suitable for the first few months of a baby's life, but after that it's crib time.

Some parents prefer to have a newborn sleep in a bassinet because of its snug size and portability, which is ideal when traveling or if the baby sleeps in your room. Bassinets also tend to be less expensive than cribs. Even if a newborn's first months are spent in a bassinet, however, within four to six months you'll have to purchase a crib because your baby probably will outgrow the bassinet. Convertible cribs that transform into daybeds, desks, or chairs can last years. Or if you like the advantages of a bassinet and a crib, look for a crib with a removable bassinet for ultimate convenience. For more information on selecting a crib, see pages 164–165.

toddler

Once your little one begins to crawl, walk, and explore the world, life is an adventure. It's only fitting, then, that a toddler's bedroom be filled with all of the elements that make childhood fun. Select a comfortable bed, sturdy furnishings, and ample toy storage first. Then choose kid-friendly colors and themes befitting your child's curiosity and boundless energy.

creative camp

SPACE TO PLAY. A toddler's room is a place for many activities—naps, storytime, and learning are only a few. High on the list of must-haves for a toddler room is a place to play. Making a separate play area in the bedroom is a great way to encourage creativity (and contain the resulting untidiness). This camp-theme boys' room is topped off with a small picnic table and tepee-style tent. The table provides a spot for art projects and snacks, while the tent is ideal for playing games of make-believe. To include play space in small rooms, establish the area with a bright rug or toddler-size table.

TWO-TONE TRICKS. Wall treatments that are two-tone—variations of the same color—can make a room seem smaller or more spacious. In this room the dark green meets the lighter hue about two-thirds of the way up the wall, which visually extends the height of the room. To make a room feel cozier and to lower the appearance of a high ceiling, make the two shades meet halfway.

RUSTIC MIX (LEFT) A consistent red and white scheme unifies the striped, plaid, and solid-color materials. The bench doubles as a place to store books and stuffed animals.

ACTIVE AREA Chalkboard paint turns closet doors into a drawing canvas. A picnic table and tepee-style tent encourage toddlers to play and pretend.

bedroom safety checklist

Your child's safety is of utmost importance anytime, but particularly when he or she begins to crawl or walk. Here's a basic list of ways to keep kids' bedrooms safe.

▸ **AFFIX** shelves, bookcases, and other heavy furnishings to the walls so they won't fall if kids lean on them.

▸ **SECURE** all drapery cords and blind cords so they are out of your child's reach.

▸ **USE** childproof plastic caps for electrical sockets.

▸ **PLACE** beds away from windows or at least use window guards to prevent children from falling out.

▸ **AVOID** toy boxes that have heavy, hinged, or lockable lids, which may fall on children or trap them inside.

▸ **KEEP** fabrics away from lamps or nightlights to reduce the risk of fire.

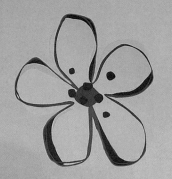

OUTDOOR SPIRIT
Flower wall stickers
coordinate with the
garden-theme bed
and nightstand, while
the bright striped
bedding lends a
contemporary touch.

flower-filled fun

GARDEN PARTY. Flowers are a popular theme for little girls' rooms. Whether the buds are bold and bright or soft and demure, the theme can easily be tailored to your child. This room features a matching bed frame and nightstand set painted to resemble a garden. Wall stickers are scattered throughout for a fanciful touch.

Stripes pick up where flowers leave off. The bright pattern on the bed, pillows, and throw rug keeps the flower theme from overpowering the space. Other decorative elements are kept to a minimum: The walls are a soft pink, and the lounging chairs are solid hues.

BUDGET-FRIENDLY FINDS. Decorating a child's room can be done without breaking the bank. Take a cue from this room. The beanbag and lounging chair, both from a large retailer, are an inexpensive way to create a reading corner. Adding a patterned rug brings character and color to ho-hum carpet. Many kids' rooms feature wall murals; the wall stickers in this room mimic the look for a fraction of the price, and they're much easier to remove.

PATTERN COMBO (RIGHT) Striped materials work well with almost any pattern, as this bed proves. Flowers and clouds coordinate with the bright striped comforter.

KEEN SCENE (RIGHT) This nightstand was purchased already adorned with the garden theme; a similar scheme could be painted on an unfinished piece of furniture.

BIGTOP BEDTIME

(ABOVE) Toddlers may hesitate when it's time to make the switch to a "big kid" bed. A fun design, like this circus train bed, may make the transition more appealing.

PLAYTIME PALS (RIGHT) A playful cast of circus characters parades along one wall of this lively bedroom.

at the circus

GO ALL OUT. Although active and energetic toddlers can be tough to keep up with, a bold and engaging bedroom will help capture their attention. Tap into one of your toddler's favorite things—a cartoon character, an animal, or a theme from make-believe—and play it up to the max. This circus-theme room was carefully thought out to ensure every detail fits with the theme. Playful wall murals set the tone with bright colors and friendly big-top characters. The theme carries over to the cozy twin-size bed, which was constructed to look like a circus train car, and the dresser that coordinates with the walls. Smaller details, such as the painted toy box and an abundance of stuffed animals, complete the theme.

PAINT POWER. Murals are an artistic way to set the scene in any room, and they're especially fun for curious toddlers. Consider hiring a professional to do the painting if you want detailed designs. Decorative painting is also a creative way to update old furniture. Before it became home to a menagerie of circus animals, the dresser in this room was an ordinary chest of drawers.

DETAILED DESIGNS (BELOW) A fabric treatment mimics a big-top tent and integrates the wall mural and dresser. Wooden animal figurines on the dresser complement the murals.

learning to share

SIBLING SPACES. When two or more kids share a room, it's important to think creatively to maximize the use of space. Children need a spot to call their own, and they also want ample room for playing together. This room illustrates an ingenious solution that balances both needs. A wall was knocked out between two bedrooms, and a large barn-style sliding door was installed in its place. During the day the three inhabitants open the door and enjoy a vast play area. At night the door slides shut; the youngest can go to sleep early while the older two continue to play or do homework quietly.

Instead of knocking down walls, you may prefer to use a temporary solution, such as a lightweight accordion-style room screen. Floor screens create partitions that can help older children concentrate on homework while little ones play. A bright throw rug can designate a play area where a younger child can keep toys and games.

CLUTTER CONTROL. With multiple children sharing one room, containing clutter takes major organization. Invest in storage pieces so kids have a place to keep books, toys, and clothes tidy. If space is tight think vertically: Hanging cubbies or shelves on a wall frees up floor space. In this room a large armoire is shared by all three boys. Although it's bigger than most children's furniture, it takes up less floor space than separate dressers might.

BOOK NOOK (ABOVE) A tall and narrow bookshelf is a good option for keeping three boys' books organized. The top shelves serve as display space for decorative items.

SPACESAVERS

(ABOVE) Deep storage cubbies fill the wall between the beds and provide ample space for books and awards. The L-shape design allows for different-size beds.

SIMPLE THROUGHOUT

(LEFT) To unify the rooms, blue is used for all the walls, bedding, and some of the furniture. The shade is also age-neutral—not too young or too old.

OPEN SPACES When the sliding door is open, the play area expands. The room design is flexible: In the future the space can be a large study or an office and a guest room.

YOUNGER SIDE

(RIGHT) Half of the large space is a 2-year-old's nursery. The sliding room divider creates a quiet spot that caters to the youngest boy's need for naps and early bedtimes.

EASY ENTRANCES (BELOW) Each room has its own entrance, convenient for when the sliding door is shut. The large sliding door was custom-made by combining three standard-size doors.

shared spaces

Kids form personal tastes early, so consider these tips when distinct personalities share a room.

▶ **MIX AND MATCH.** Allow for individuality in kids' separate areas. A simple wall treatment creates a subtle backdrop so individual color preferences can be displayed in bedding and accessories.

▶ **CREATE ZONES.** If two children share a bedroom, create three zones: one for each sibling and one area that's shared space. Use folding screens to decoratively separate areas.

▶ **STAY ORGANIZED.** With more than one kid in a room, storage can be difficult. Avoid mix-ups by designating distinct drawers, bins, and other storage items for each child. To free up space consider storage pieces that can slide under the bed or a window seat that lifts up and doubles as a toy box.

SOFT SPOTS (ABOVE) An overstuffed chair is an inviting spot for reading a book before bedtime. Soft fabrics and light colors are a soothing combination to surround the bed.

A LIGHT TOUCH (BELOW) A pair of large windows allows natural light to spill into the room. Built-in shelves keep the room tidy.

timeless retreat

BALANCING ACT. Chances are much of the furniture purchased for your toddler's room is made to last well into his or her teen years. Picking classic styles for the bed, dresser, and chairs provides a blank slate that will endure trends and changes in tastes as your child grows. This room combines grown-up furniture with little-girl details. The headboard is a basic shape, while its handpainted fairy scene is fanciful. The headboard is easy to repaint if a tween girl decides fairy motifs are too childish.

Color choices at this stage can go several ways. Pastels or bold prints are appealing to this age group, but other options can work well too. The golds and yellows in this room are bright and sunny, which is perfect for toddlers. Yellow is a smart base color. It's gender-neutral, allowing kids to switch rooms down the road, and it coordinates with both soft pastels and bold primary colors.

This bedroom also uses a variety of textures. Toddlers start to pick up on different textures early—soft and cuddly bedspreads, smooth dresser drawers, and silky curtains provide visual and tactile interest for curious tots.

DAINTY DETAILS

Lacy trim on the pillows, lamp, and bedskirt adds a girlish touch to the classic furniture. The handpainted fairy scene on the headboard is a tasteful yet youthful focal point.

STAR COMMAND

With a little canvas and imagination, this bed doubles as a fort where a little boy can play astronaut. A slide adds an extra dose of fun to the room.

PLUSH PLANET

(RIGHT) A soft planet-shape pillow tops off the theme. Along with space-inspired bedding and finials, a vintage-look poster adds quirky charm.

out of this world

PLANETARY PLAY. A small room can still include big-time fun as long as you use space wisely. Look for opportunities to combine necessary elements—for example, the bed in this room is a sleep area and play space all in one. Red canvas panels and a tent transform the underbed space into a fort, while a slide tops off the play center. The best part is that it all fits into one compact corner, leaving plenty of space elsewhere in the room for other necessary furnishings.

STELLAR DETAILS. With a few fun details, any room can be transformed from four blank walls to imagination central. The outer-space theme here began with the planet wall stickers, which are easily removable. The stickers pop against bright but basic blue paint. The theme also carries over to the bed and play area. Bright planet-shape finials on each of the four bedposts stand out against the maple finish. Finials for child-size beds come in many shapes, making them an easy way to incorporate a theme.

SOLAR SPIN (BELOW) Wall stickers are an easy way to add character to a room and are less permanent than a mural. These are removed with a little water, so they won't damage walls.

JUST RIGHT (RIGHT)
Round bulletin boards
and a mirror are hung
low so a child can reach
them. The chair adds a
funky touch and is easy
for kids to climb on
and off.

CREATIVE STORAGE (BELOW) This
bookshelf is a thrift store find. With a little
paint, cutouts for windows, and a triangle
roof, it resembles a dollhouse, complete
with a fun clock for learning to tell time.

bright
ideas

BEDROOM ESSENTIALS. While plenty
of the furniture in a toddler's room can
be adapted and reused over the years,
it may be useful to include a few age-
appropriate items. A toddler acquires
possessions quickly—books, toys, art
supplies—so ample storage space is
necessary. Teaching young children to
clean up after themselves will be easier
if the storage space is accessible to
them. The dollhouse-inspired bookshelf
in this room is a fun twist on a basic
storage piece, and its open design and low
height are just right for a toddler to put
things away.

Also consider adding toddler-size
furniture, like the small lime green chair
featured here. Furniture that's low to the
ground is ideal; small children can easily
climb on and off a chair built for them,
but they'll struggle if an adult-size chair
or table is added to the room too early.

SPACESAVER. It may be tempting
to invest in a full-size bed; however,
having more play room may be a better
use of space while children are young.
If sleepovers are likely in a few years,
consider a twin-size trundle bed. Here the
beaded-board bed frame looks as though
it includes storage drawers. Instead it
hides a second mattress that easily pulls
out for friends to use.

FLOWER POWER
Accent pieces convey a bold flower theme. Accessories can be switched out if tastes change in a few years.

update furniture with paint

Paint can energize furniture in much the same way it enlivens walls. Use a single hue or go all out with decorative touches to update your pieces.

Whether you're painting a brand-new, unfinished piece of furniture or repurposing furnishings that have already been finished, you'll need to prep the surface before you paint. Thoroughly clean the piece and then lightly sand the wood in the direction of the grain. Particularly when refinishing old pieces, you may need to fill in gaps or cracks with wood filler. Allow it to dry completely, sand the filled areas, and remove any dust with a tack cloth. The next step is to prime the furniture. Once the primer is completely dry, apply a finish coat (for one-color application) or a base color (for decorative painting). Refer to pages 134–143 for more information on using color and paint in kids' rooms.

in the sea

SMALL-SCALE SAILING. A room with small square footage can hold everything a young child needs. This modestly proportioned space includes all the necessities—a comfortable bed, plenty of storage for books and toys, grown-up and kid-size chairs for storytime, and a desk area—and boasts a colorful, stimulating nautical theme too. Primary-color fabric with a vibrant pattern featuring various types of sea life is perfect for a child who loves the ocean and its inhabitants. The fabric adorns everything from the bed and window seat cushions to the bulletin board above the desk.

ADDING DETAIL. One way to add interest to any room in the house is to incorporate architectural detail. In this room made for a young sailor, thick white trimwork around windows and doors pairs with beaded-board wainscoting on the walls for a beachy look. A sailboat wallpaper border above the chair rail adds more eye-catching detail. The all-white furnishings blend with the white wainscoting to make the small space seem larger and brighter. The bed and bookshelf incorporate panels that look like wainscoting, and the storage benches beneath the windows are made to look like built-in window seats.

SEAWORTHY STORAGE (ABOVE)
A bookcase occupies the spot between the windows and is flanked by fun storage boxes that double as window seats. Lift-up lids for storage boxes should be light enough that they won't injure children reaching in for toys.

GONE FISHIN' (BELOW)
For a twist on the standard child-size chair, this tiny rocker with a sailboat back, oversize fish arms, and "wave" rockers enhances the nautical motif.

FUTURE NEEDS

Although a toddler might not use a desk all that often, it provides a spot for drawing or playing educational computer games now and will come in handy for doing homework in a few years.

PERFECT BLEND
Browns combine to create an earthy feel. The vertical stripes on the wall make the ceiling seem higher, and the neutral tones allow the red accent pieces to stand out.

howdy, partner

PATTERN PARADE. Whether you choose to stick with a simple theme or mix and match a variety of prints, a toddler's room is a fun place to experiment with patterns. This cowboy room embraces vertical and horizontal stripes, spots, check prints, and cowhide-inspired fabrics. To prevent the mix from overwhelming the space, the walls are painted in earthy tones, and the flooring, toy box, and nightstand are left their natural wood hues. Choosing to accentuate one color—like the red of the armchair, bed, and accessories—also helps unify a room.

Sometimes one piece can be an inspiration. This polka-dot rug with brown, black, and red circles was the starting point for the color palette. It helps to designate one element—such as the rug—as the reference for a color or pattern scheme to ensure individual elements will coordinate in the completed room.

CHECKPOINT (RIGHT)
The check window treatments add a subtle, small-scale pattern to the mix. The black pattern also coordinates with the black spots on the rug.

STUCK TO YOU

A large magnetic board draws little ones to play with alphabet magnets. It's a nice alternative to traditional bulletin boards because there are no sharp tacks.

ANIMAL ELEMENT
(LEFT) The cushions on this vintage chair were reupholstered with cowhide fabric, which adds a funky twist.

ALL-STAR (RIGHT) Fun star-shape hooks coordinate with the cowboy theme and color scheme. Placed next to the door, they're also a practical place to hang jackets.

SLEEK STORAGE (BELOW) Cubbies are hung high above the magnetic board. Besides adding a decorative element to the room, the cubbies keep objects out of reach of little hands.

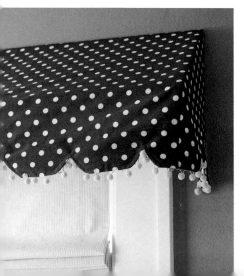

DOTTY DESIGN

(LEFT) The polka-dot window treatments were designed to resemble bakeshop awnings. Chocolate brown and icing pink are a bold take on vintage design.

SWEET DREAMS

(ABOVE) Tiny felt cupcakes slide out of their pockets on the bedspread. The heirloom bed frame and nightstand add a nostalgic touch.

PRETTY IN PINK Stripes of pink and white run through the entire room. The retro scalloped edges on the blackboard mimic similar details on the nightstand, shelves, and window treatments.

CHEF'S CHOICE (ABOVE) Baking sheets transform into magnetic boards, and rolling pins become accessory racks. Bookshelf curtains make it easy to hide clutter.

vintage vibes

TIME TRAVELERS. Look to the past for decorating inspiration and you'll never run short on ideas. This girl's room takes on a 1950s bakery theme, sweetly carried out with retro details. Vintage design can be bright and bold or quiet and classic, depending on what theme you choose. After researching the time period, head to antiques shops and flea markets to find authentic items or consider including pieces that have been passed down in your family to add special meaning. Before any used furniture is placed in a toddler's room, check that it is in good condition and safe for children.

SITTING PRETTY (LEFT) Upholstered in a soft green, this refurbished '40s boudoir chair is a curvy counterpoint to the stripes and checks theme.

CHEERFUL PATTERNS (BELOW) Lime green paired with yellow and red accents gives this room a tangy and energetic feel that's perfect for a toddler.

practical details

PLANNING FOR PRECOCIOUSNESS.
When little ones transition into the
toddler stage, curiosity is sure to follow.
A well-planned room can allow a toddler
to have fun while keeping trouble to a
minimum. This room uses white wall
shelves hung 2 feet below the ceiling
to keep decorative objects out of reach.
The shelves are also a good way to save
space if the floor plan is tight. The bed
features curved sides that look cool and
may prevent a child from falling out
while asleep. Look for a bed that can
accommodate guardrails if you'd like
more security.

DECORATING UNDERFOOT. Hardy
flooring is convenient in a toddler's
room. As long as no one in the family
has allergies, choosing carpet may be a
budget-friendly option. This carpeting
boasts a neutral hue; however, many
different colors and patterns are
available. Wool-synthetic blends are a
common choice because they're durable,
affordable, and available in many designs.
Some carpets are even stain-resistant for
the inevitable spills in a toddler's room.

COLOR COMBO (BELOW) The neutral
walls, bed, and cabinet keep the bright
patterns on the windows and pillows
from overwhelming the space.

tween

No longer little kids but not quite grown, tweens are serious about what they want in their bedrooms. Bolder colors, personal touches, and grown-up furnishings are key. Include elements that will last through your child's teen years. At the same time remember that in this space personal interests—from music to drama to spending time with friends—should take center stage.

 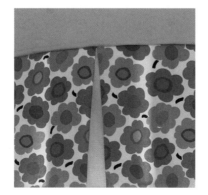 

CONSTANT COLOR (LEFT) The green and pink theme is carried out at every level. Fabrics display the colors in stripes, flowers, and polka dots, while vintage furniture lends a retro vibe to the scheme.

major impact

COLOR CHOICES. Tweens may want color combos that you would never dream of pairing. It's worth considering the far-out choices though. Here the lime green and hot pink decor is a strong combination that achieves a cheerful, vintage look. If you're not ready to go all out, keep walls and furnishings toned down and let your child pick strong-colored accents.

EASY ILLUMINATION. When a bedroom needs a boost of light, unique and creative lamps, sconces, and fixtures are practical and fun. A ceiling fixture can shed light on most of the room, while sconces and lamps may be used for task lighting at a desk or bed. Many styles are available, so choose whatever works best with your design scheme.

The lighting choices in this room have a funky, whimsical style. Bases on the desk and bedside lamps feature interesting shapes, while the fringe on the ceiling fixture adds an unexpected twist. Lampshades alone add impact and can jazz up an old lamp base. When shopping for a lampshade, take the base with you so you can see how they look together.

TRENDY STUDYING (ABOVE) The study area boasts a variety of funky elements, from the hanging display cubes to the distressed desk. The vintage desk chair was reupholstered with faux fur, and a sleek magnetic board is handy for posting notes.

DOUBLE DUTY
(RIGHT) An open storage unit fits perfectly in the window nook. With a few pillows it mimics a built-in window seat and is an ideal spot for both storing and reading books.

TWO-TONE FRESHNESS (ABOVE)
Painting the large dresser two shades of pink adds visual interest. The iron bed frame was originally white. Now a few coats of bright green paint give it a fresh, vibrant look.

update walls with paint

Painted walls make an easily changeable statement and add instant personality.

Your tween informs you that she needs new color in her room. Now. Aside from swapping bedding, window treatments, and accessories, painting the walls is one of the easiest ways to go all out with color—without regretting it later. If your child convinces you to go for a bright hue on all the walls, paint the ceiling and moldings in the room white or neutral so the color scheme is less jarring. Are you hesitant to go bold on all the walls? Compromise by allowing her to pick the color for an accent wall, and then paint the other walls a neutral or complementary hue. That way when your tween decides hot pink is out and lime green is in, repainting will be easier. Turn to pages 134–143 for more paint tips and tricks.

BOB WHO? Framed rock-icon artwork is an easy, inexpensive alternative to the standard headboard.

rock 'n' roll

BACKSTAGE PASS. Keeping a makeover with a theme under control is as easy as limiting the color scheme to subdued hues. The walls and bedding in this room—dominated by earth tones with contrasting black and navy—set the stage for a harmonic space filled with red and silver accessories. Music-note wallpaper adorns the lower half of the walls below the white-painted chair rail, creating a subtle surround-sound effect. It makes for serious style for a tween who's hip to tunes. To complete the scene inexpensive black frames ensure displayed posters hit a high note with parents and kids alike; it's easy to swap posters as music tastes change.

ROCKIN' RED (BELOW) A red metal cabinet and silver accessories add a bit of edginess to the otherwise neutral color scheme.

IT'S A HIT (RIGHT)
Music-note fabric and CDs applied to a custom valance command the spotlight in a room with serious rhythm.

WELL-TUNED The colors of the bedding are neutral, while a mix of patterns keeps things interesting.

SECRET SPACES

(ABOVE) A staircase inside the bedroom leads to a small loft area perfect for games, reading, or listening to music. Built-in shelves underneath provide practical storage.

BASIC BORDERS

(RIGHT) White beaded board surrounds the room below the mural. Beaded board adds an interesting architectural detail that can pair with solid-color or patterned wallpaper when the mural is replaced.

whimsical transition

STRIKING A BALANCE. When planning a tween bedroom, it's tough to know whether you should cater to your child's younger characteristics or her more mature instincts. You can do both with a few simple choices that make it easy to adjust to changing tastes. This room caters to a child's little-girl side with pink hues, frilly details, and a fanciful wall mural. Yet it's easy to transform the room into a more grown-up space. The walls may be painted, or if the mural stays, new accessories might give it a completely different feel. For example, the bedspread and pillows can be traded out for ones with deeper tones so the mural will look less fairy-tale and more mysterious.

Lamps and window treatments are an easy way to change the tone of any room. The windows in this space let in lots of sunshine; in a few years, long curtains, blinds, or shades can create different moods.

BUILT-IN ADAPTABILITY (ABOVE) For now the built-in window seat is home to stuffed animals. In a few years the countertop can be a vanity, and the window seat can be a spot for chatting with friends.

FLUTTERY FINISH (RIGHT) Butterflies pick up where the wall murals stop, adorning the soft draperies. The window treatments allow plenty of sunshine to spill into the room.

WALL FLOWER (ABOVE) The vines and flowers on the walls were painted freehand using a variety of brushes. Stencils would also produce a perfect floral flourish.

FRIENDLY FACE (BELOW) A smiling hula dancer is reflected in the mirror above the dresser. For an added embellishment silk hibiscus blooms were hot-glued to the unframed glass.

tropical paradise

HAWAIIAN FLAIR. When you're creating a room with a theme, the fun lies in the details. Begin with the right combination of colors, fabrics, and furnishings; then add some well-placed tchotchkes to infuse a space with personality. Use some restraint when adding accessories to avoid creating clutter. In this tropical tween room, walls painted with flowers in splashy hues, large fabric leaf fronds, a woven window shade, and leaf-shape fan blades set the scene. The little details—including a flower-shape rug, hula-dancer dolls, and silk blooms—finish the space in style.

PRACTICAL PAINT. Use a large-scale motif to frame pieces of furniture. At first glance the vines of island blooms on these walls may merely look like pretty paintings. However, they were actually strategically placed to help anchor furnishings, including the desk and dresser.

ISLE OF STYLE The woven furnishings will last long after a child's love for splashy island colors fades. A full-size bed is a smart investment that pays off as a tween grows into a teen.

CORNER COURT (LEFT) A basketball hoop brings outdoor fun inside. Handpainted storage lockers are functional and fit the theme. Pillows and artwork round out the corner.

team huddle

SPORTY BLEND (BELOW) A custom-made World Series banner is a big contribution to the sport theme. Although the quilt does not have a sports motif, its plaid pattern blends well with the color scheme.

TIMELESS THEMES. Sometimes children's tastes come and go as fast as the kids grow, and that can be a challenge if you're trying to decorate for longevity. Some themes, however, will stand the test of time. Take this boy's sports-theme room: The idea is broad, so it's easy to adapt the room as a child's sports preferences change. Green walls with decorative stripes near the ceiling set a basic palette. Unpainted furnishings were purchased from a local store and then painted to blend with the colors in the room.

The backdrop is basic, and the fun game details will be easy to change down the road. A bedside lamp combines a few sports, including soccer and basketball, in its base. Custom pieces, such as the banner hanging over the bed and the valance, make strong statements and up the fun factor in the room.

USEFUL ITEMS. Thematic elements can appear on items as small as pillows or as large as major storage pieces. In this room lockers were handpainted and distressed to fit the sports theme. In addition to the unique lockers, shelves and a chest of drawers (shown on page 74) help keep the room tidy.

This bed illustrates the importance of keeping large items basic and catering to current tastes through details. The frame and quilt will last for years, while the sports-inspired pillows can be switched out.

WALL SPACE Basics and details mix on this wall devoted to storage. The wood furnishings have a warm tone, while details such as football bookends and baseball picture frames pop against the backdrop.

GAME TIME Striped curtain panels featuring a broad denim hem complement the colors of the quilt on the nearby bed.

TOUCHDOWN DESIGN
(LEFT) Cutouts of footballs, baseballs, basketballs, and soccer balls are a lively mix on the window valance designed to reflect the sports interests of the boy who resides in this room.

EASY CHANGE
(RIGHT) Playful pillows enliven the bed. The fuchsia satin comforter is reversible—with a quick flip, orange becomes the new color of the moment.

glamour & glitz

TIME TO SHINE. A decorating scheme that works for a quiet, mellow child will probably be different from one that fits a rambunctious, extroverted kid. Before updating a tween room, consider the child's personality and tastes. In this case a glamorous Hollywood-theme room with a punchy palette of hot pinks and aquas is exactly what a bubbly, outgoing girl requires. Shaggy star-shape rugs, feather boas, and a personalized director's chair (see page 79) are star-quality details that ensure the room fits a diva in the making.

ACT TWO. Toddler toys may be a thing of the past, but even tweens enjoy a room with space for play. Tailor play spaces to your child's interests. The dream element in this room is a stage for performing, complete with a pink karaoke machine and rocker-girl guitar (shown on page 78). A drawer on one side of the stage stores dress-up clothes, a vanity provides a spot for primping, and plenty of mirrors ensure the star of the show is ready to go before taking the stage.

PLACE TO PREEN (BELOW) This classic vanity doubles as a spot for homework. For added star style paper lanterns clipped to the mirror mimic makeup lights.

STRIKE A POSE

(LEFT) Mirrored oval detailing on the armoire adds glitz and provides an additional place for primping. Star-studded accessories on the armoire double as props for playtime.

DREAM RETREAT

(ABOVE) This beaded canopy bed is many tween girls' dream come true. The canopy fabric can be swapped out if tween tastes change.

STAR SETTING

(ABOVE) The stage—complete with a karaoke machine, guitar, and Walk of Fame plaque—launched the Hollywood design theme. The curtains can close between acts.

ACTION! (RIGHT) Thoughtful details make a big impact in a theme room—as these accessories prove.

HOT PINK Pink rules in this star-studded room, which includes a pint-size recliner and a feather-trimmed phone. A pink curtain covers the nightstand's oval cutout so clutter is out of sight.

CLOSEUP TIME (RIGHT) A bright pink personalized director's chair draped with a feather boa is a must in a room brimming with Hollywood style.

living with a theme

A theme room doesn't have to live with you forever. Consider these tips for creating a space with staying power.

▶ **SPEND WISELY.** Splurge on the key pieces that will outlast the theme, such as furniture with classic style and solid-color fabrics.

▶ **LOOK FOR VERSATILITY.** Furniture that serves multiple functions—a vanity that doubles as a desk, for instance—ensures maximum flexibility. A reversible comforter is another option that will let you quickly change a look.

▶ **KEEP BACKDROPS SIMPLE.** Rather than hanging wallpaper or stenciling a motif that plays up a child's latest craze, keep the walls simple to avoid a major do-over. Let the accessories, not the walls, convey the theme.

BRIGHT IDEA (ABOVE) A creative way to make a statement, the citrus-hue lights above the desk are actually inexpensive kitchen pendants.

all about orange

JUICY COLOR. On the verge of their teen years, preteens often long for a dose of bold color. In fact, ask savvy tweens to pick their favorite colors, and a juicy orange hue much like the one on these walls may top their list. The bursts of bright color in this room continue in the fabrics and accessories; careful color selection ensures its attitude isn't overwhelming. Solid colors—such as the teal shag rug and the yellow bedding—provide a somewhat subdued backdrop, allowing floral fabrics to take the lead role on the windows. In such a bold room, color and patterns need not match perfectly, though they'll look best if they coordinate.

RECYCLED STYLE. There's no need to start from scratch when designing a tween room—in fact, with a few smart additions and subtractions, many of the elements that currently occupy your child's room can become tween basics. Here, for example, a convertible crib takes the form of a moon-shape chair, a changing table transforms into a desk, and a bookshelf loses some shelves and gains two doors to serve as an armoire.

DISPLAY CENTRAL (LEFT) Painted cork squares turn this wall into a functional, stylish bulletin board.

FRIENDLY BED
A big bed loaded with comfy pillows is perfect for long gabfests with girlfriends.

STOWAWAY (LEFT)
A deep armoire stores all the clothing a tween girl needs. Peel-and-stick dots dress up the door.

RAINBOW BRIGHT
(RIGHT) These custom Roman shades were a splurge. However, the striped fabric was a good investment that allows for a rainbow of color possibilities.

IN CIRCLES Nature and geometry collide in this tiny tween room: The duvet sports colorful trees, dragonfly lights adorn the shelf, and bold circles appear above and below the bed in the paintings and rugs.

ALL WHITE (BELOW) Perhaps the best color for opening up a room, bright white adorns the walls and dresser.

FLY AWAY (BELOW) The dragonfly theme continues on the dresser. A fabric-covered corkboard on the wall is perfect for displaying mementos.

OPEN DESIGN (RIGHT)
The clean lines and open design of the metal desk and chair allow a clear view to the outside. A mirrored closet door makes the space appear even roomier.

pretty & personal

PERFECT FIT. Even tiny bedrooms can boast serious style when the furnishings are arranged to maximize available space. Placing the low platform bed, sleek metal desk and chair, and white locker-style dresser against the walls in this tiny tween room leaves space for kids to sprawl in the middle of the floor. White walls and light carpet further the illusion of a larger room, as does the large window adorned only with sheer pink curtains to take advantage of natural light.

PERSONAL TOUCH. For an inexpensive and creative way to adorn the walls, consider making your own artwork. Splash some paint on a canvas, or print and frame a funky photo. The glowing dragonfly lights and the colors of the duvet cover in this room inspired the homemade paintings on the wall above the bed. Children may want to create their own artwork for the walls. Include a fabric-covered bulletin board like the one above the dresser so they'll have a spot to display additional creations.

small room, spacious style

Use these tricks to make a small room look bigger.

▸ **PAINT WALLS** in light colors with cool undertones. Pale greens and blues are good choices for opening up a space.

▸ **USE COLORS** similar to the wall color for fabrics, patterns, and furniture so these items fade into the background.

▸ **PLACE FURNITURE** that is larger against the longest wall. This will draw attention away from the smaller parts of the room.

▸ **AVOID SHADOWS** by adding soft lights. Use gauzy fabric for window treatments or leave windows uncovered.

▸ **MAINTAIN OPEN SPACES.** The farther you can see into or through a space, the larger it will seem. Avoid blocking views to windows and doors and leave some open floor space.

teen

When it comes to teen rooms, your teen can tell you the only phrase that truly matters: "It's all about me." Perhaps your teen yearns for luxurious fabrics or hot hues. Or maybe a suite with distinctive areas for sleeping and seating is in order. Collaborate with your teen on a design strategy and get ready for a wild ride through teen style.

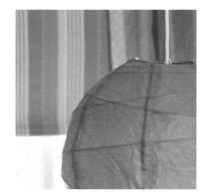

hot hues, cool ideas

COLOR RULES. Energetic teens require equally energetic design in their personal spaces. Finding the right mix of bold color without going overboard requires careful consideration. This room gets it right by setting the scene with subdued wood floors, pale green walls, and white trimwork. These choices balance the bold orange and pink hues and multitude of patterns layered in the space. Creative uses of fabric and color stand out—for instance, the inset panel of the built-in cabinetry is painted a vibrant pink, and Roman shades in a graphic pattern cover the windows and built-in bookshelf.

MULTIUSE. In true teen-suite style, the room features distinct functional spaces, including seating areas for talking with friends, a workspace, and a comfortable bed.

PRICE-CONSCIOUS
The custom headboard and bedding were made from reasonably priced fabrics. Inexpensive artwork from local stores provides the finishing touch.

SIT HERE (LEFT) A fuzzy rug defines a cozy conversation area with two orange barrel-back chairs, an oversize ottoman, and a clear side table.

THOUGHTFUL ADDITION (ABOVE) The border added to the orange quilted coverlet comes from the fabric used for the Roman shades.

IT WORKS (BELOW) These once-unfinished furnishings received a dose of personality with custom painting. Artwork framed in black anchors the room.

ON DISPLAY (ABOVE) Removing the shelves from a built-in bookshelf created a display niche near the bed. The painted stripes draw the niche into the color scheme.

WHAT A SPOT An old love seat with a zebra-print slipcover and a pair of pink suede cubes at the foot of the bed distinguish another seating area. Reproduction artwork ups the ante on personality in this room.

CUSTOM SEATING

(ABOVE) Numerical decals mark the boy's birth date on the back of his desk chair. The desk and chair fit neatly under a full-size loft bed and provide a spot to complete homework.

SIMPLE STYLE (ABOVE) Minimalist furniture, such as the sleek loft bed and black chairs, balances the bold colors on the ceiling and walls.

SHADED STRIPES

(ABOVE) A five-color palette gives the room a retro vibe. The stripes run throughout the room near the floor and ceiling. A block of blue between the stripes keeps the room light.

STYLISH SHELVES
(RIGHT) A steel and maple bookcase is modern and will be well used for years to come. For now it provides plenty of space for books, photos, and favorite items.

lofty living

GAME ZONE (BELOW) A steel TV stand is anchored into the wall from behind and connected to both the floor and ceiling, allowing it to be turned either way for better viewing.

THINKING AHEAD. Once kids hit the teen years, they'll graduate before you know it and move out on their own. Redecorating a teen's room is a great time to invest in some pieces that children can take with them when they move into the dorms or their own apartment. This boy's room is filled with modern basics that would look cool in any environment. From the sleek bookcase to the comfy black chairs and ottomans, the styles are durable and timeless. A lofted bed like this silver one is useful too because it frees up floor space for more fun, funky elements beside the practical ones.

PERSONALIZED HANGOUT. Tailoring decor to a teen's tastes is sure to please. The one-of-a-kind tie-dye ceiling in this bedroom was created using spray paint. The ceiling colors coordinate with the retro-style stripes that run along the top and bottom of the walls. A love of video games inspired a media area complete with TV, game systems, and chairs—perfect for having friends over to hang out. Quirky details—such as the clock-face table between the gaming chairs—give the room even more personality.

DANGLING DIVIDER

(RIGHT) Hanging plastic rings create a fun curtain between the bedroom and adjoining bathroom. The cool blue tones coordinate with an accent rug and one of the wall panels.

BOLD DESIGN

(BELOW) Funky accessories, such as a contemporary clock and geometric table lamp, add a punch of color near the love seat.

lounging around

CARVING OUT SPACE. Teenagers have a lot going on in their lives: School, friendships, and after-school activities are only a few of the things on their minds. Creating a bedroom that sets aside space for different functions is one way to help them organize it all. This bedroom delineates three areas: one for sleeping, one for hosting friends, and another for doing homework (not shown). The section made for hanging out with friends is filled with bright, minimalist furnishings. A lime green love seat sets the pace and provides a comfy spot for flipping through magazines.

The sleeping area is a bit more subdued. Light-color wood gives the bed and nightstand a simple, peaceful look. Instead of a headboard, dangly discs hang along the wall, adding shine and interest. To create separate spaces in a teen room, consider using floor rugs to define an area or selecting different color palettes for each space.

WALL POWER. With so many possible color combos and finishes, it's easy to make a statement with walls. This room uses several blocks of color, tied together by the same paint technique. When the paint was still wet, a cloth was used to create a soft mottled texture. Different paint techniques can create moods ranging from sophisticated to edgy—it all depends on your and your child's tastes.

LIGHTEN UP (ABOVE) Furnishings in the sleeping area are light-toned to keep the room feeling open and airy. The lamp and hanging strands add interesting detail to the space.

BRIGHT SIGHT
Vibrant colors establish a fun mood in the social area of the room. The love seat is perfectly scaled for a bedroom lounging area.

BOARDED UP (ABOVE) Old skateboards with their wheels removed form a one-of-a-kind headboard. Solid-color bedding ensures the focus is on the funky boards.

SPOT COLOR
A distressed red desk unit breaks up the blue and brown color scheme. It also provides ample space to keep books handy, spread out homework, and talk on the phone.

gnarly hangout

ATTIC AREAS. Teens seeking more privacy may request a move to the attic. At first the slanting ceilings and oddly shaped nooks and crannies may seem like a series of design challenges. But as this bold teenage boy's room shows, embracing the unusual dimensions of the space can have a big payoff.

Posters of varying sizes and designs hang on the ceiling and accentuate the angles, while blues and deep browns cover the walls. If you'd like to make an attic seem larger, stick to light-color paints and fabrics. The odd under-the-eaves space in this room (shown on page 97) was turned into a tiki-theme private nook. Shag carpet, beanbags, a lava lamp, and a bamboo-bead door combine to create a funky hangout.

AGED APPEAL. Here's some good news: For most teens brand-new is not a necessity. In fact, a few vintage or distressed pieces can add a cool, casual, and comfortable feel to the room. A plain desk unit was painted distressed red, bringing both brightness and character to the space. Old skateboards—complete with scuffs and scratches—were used to fashion a headboard. The same concept can be applied to other hobbies to give use to old equipment: A worn-out baseball glove, old guitar picks, or outgrown jerseys can all be artfully displayed to reflect your child's interests.

BALANCE GAME

Because the ceiling is plastered with an array of posters, the furnishings in this teen boy's room are kept relatively simple.

CORNER POCKET A reading chair is situated under a window and below a lamp for lots of light. Details like a vintage bowling pin turned hat stand add character.

STYLE MIX (RIGHT)
Eclectic posters and a classic-looking chandelier are a fun mix of styles. Of course, the chandelier also provides light, which is critical if an attic room is short on windows.

HIP HIDEAWAY
(BELOW) With a flame-painted ceiling, comfy beanbags, and bamboo beads, an awkward nook is transformed into a cool hangout.

SIMPLE SPOT A bath next to the bedroom is intentionally understated—in a few years it will be a guest bathroom. Details such as a skateboard and stuffed monkey lend a personal touch.

COLOR COMBO A sleek bed frame and light walls anchor the bold mix of reds, oranges, and magentas. The result is a cheerful, comfy oasis.

SPOT ON (LEFT) This window treatment boasts a big dose of personality. Felt cutouts connected by monofilament dangle in front of a semisheer white shade.

RED ALL 'ROUND (RIGHT) The funky red chair is a strong addition to the circle theme. It's also a great spot for chatting on the phone or reading.

retro retreat

CURVY CUES. Going retro can be a fun project for you and your teen. Retro style can take innumerable forms, so decide on a unifying theme—a color, shape, or style—early on. This room features circle-inspired accessories, which combine to create an energetic, mod hangout. From a dotty window treatment to a round red chair, circular shapes rule in this groovy room.

Often a theme can be carried out through details alone. Here round magnetic boards, a curved-edge desk chair, and a wavy-print bedspread make sure the message gets across loud and clear. The powder blue walls and hardwood floors could have just as easily grounded rock star-, ocean-, or art-inspired themes, proving theme decorating really is all in the details.

SOFTER SIDE. Teens want more than a place to call their own; they want the spot to be comfy too. This room adds soft touches using a variety of textures. A fuzzy rug warms up the hardwood floor around the bed, while pillows of various sizes and shapes are plentiful.

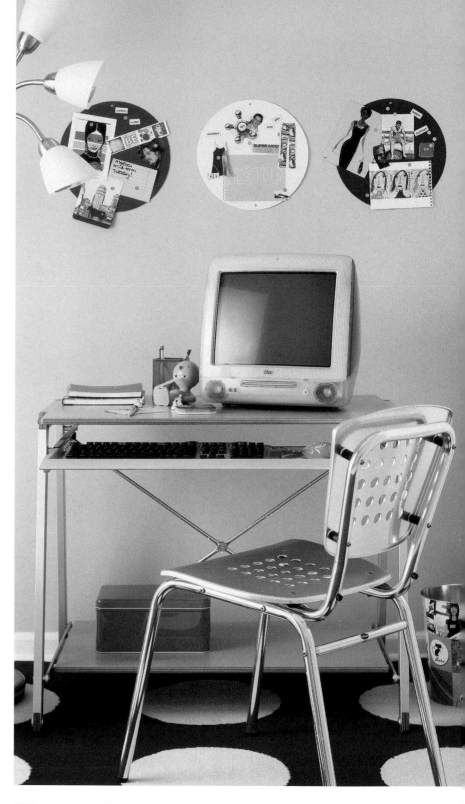

JAZZY WORKSTATION
(ABOVE) A cool desk and fun accessories make completing homework a bit more bearable. The round magnetic boards hold reminders of upcoming tests and magazine clippings. Practical but funky, the lamp provides plenty of light.

LOOK UP The sweet-dreams canopy above the bed was made by sewing a band of fabric around a 45-inch square of sheer organdy. It's attached to the ceiling hooks with ribbons.

BRIGHT COVER

(LEFT) For a touch of personality, this lampshade was covered with silk fabric and other embellishments, including beads and handcrafted butterflies.

SINKING IN

(BELOW) Piles of pillows in coordinating colors add sink-in luxury on the velvet-upholstered love seat.

living in luxury

FUN WITH FABRICS. Designing a luxurious retreat for your teen can be affordable—as long as you're willing to do some work. The sumptuous fabrics and frills in this teen room create a decadent hideaway that, upon closer inspection, is actually a do-it-yourself dream. Most of the elements in the room—including the canopy above the bed, the box bedspread, and the window treatments, pillows, and lampshades—are easy to make once you've selected a variety of fabric colors, patterns, and textures.

SET THE SCENE. A subdued backdrop ensures textiles steal the show. Here soft gray walls and white trimwork serve as a neutral setting for the fabrics and the sunny yellow furniture. Sanding the painted parquet floor and coating it with polyurethane created an aged-linen look that grounds the design.

LEFTOVERS (ABOVE)
Fabric scraps from other projects in the room make stylish throw pillows. Different pillow shapes and sizes add contrast.

ON THE BOTTOM (RIGHT)
Below the box bedspread a sheer bedskirt banded with plaid silk adds a casual, light touch.

mixing
patterns

Pick three patterns for harmony in any decorating scheme.

You know a room that deftly incorporates a multitude of patterns when you see it, but how do you mix patterns in your own spaces without creating a dull collection of small prints or an overabundance of large ones? The key lies in starting with one print you love and working in color-related fabrics in two other scales. Then for unity and balance, spread the chosen patterns throughout the space. The room on pages 100–103 is a perfect example—the large, feminine floral on the bed mixes with the midsize stripe on the Roman shade and the smaller-scale plaid on the bedskirt and canopy for a luxe design that impresses without overwhelming.

THE STRIPES HAVE IT (LEFT) Ribbons of varying widths add texture and color to an otherwise standard Roman shade.

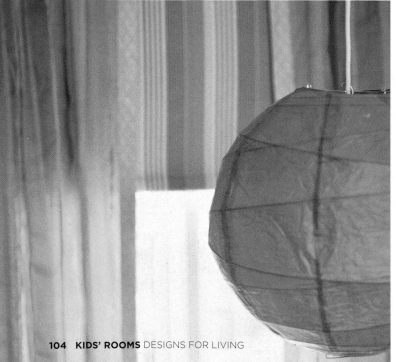

BRIGHT SPOTS

(ABOVE) Painted storage
cubbies add a sense
of depth to the attic
room and combine with
pillows and a bedside
lamp for serious flair.

COLOR COLUMNS (LEFT) Sheer turquoise
fabric layered over bold multicolor stripes
creates a one-of-a-kind window treatment.
A paper lantern tops off the cheerful spirit of
this space.

TEXTURE MIX (RIGHT)
Pillows are a must in any teen's room. These combine different textures and colors with fuzzy materials and dangly details.

STANDOUT STYLE
(RIGHT) An orange chair and ottoman pop against white walls, light flooring, and a glass table.

splashes of color

VIBRANT VARIETY. When your teen wants to decorate with psychedelic colors and you want a room that stands the test of time, compromise is easier than it seems. This room has plenty of zest and a few neutrals too. Because the room is in an attic, the walls were painted a bright white to make it appear larger. The same concept applies for the blond furnishings.

When larger elements are in neutral tones, even small bursts of color have a major effect. The built-in storage cubbies above the bed are an immediate focal point, thanks to vibrant paint colors on the interior of each cube. Inexpensive accessories such as paper lanterns, throw rugs, and pillows also up the brightness factor in any room.

transitions

It's a fact: Children grow up quickly. Even if they're rapidly outgrowing their clothing, however, their rooms can grow with them. Select hardworking, versatile furnishings and a classic color scheme to ensure your child's room fits from one life stage to the next. Then all you have to do is swap out the accessories to achieve a fresh look.

STORAGE SPOT

(RIGHT) A built-in, which includes drawers under the window seat and bookshelves, provides lots of storage.

ready for a change

EASY MOVE. With a little planning your child's room can be designed to adapt to his or her increasing maturity. This little girl's room was built with a toddler in mind, yet the space can easily become a teen room, thanks to classic white-painted furnishings and a hip color scheme.

A plaid bedspread and a coordinating lime and pink quilt were the inspiration for the color palette. Fabrics with similar hues and distinctive patterns add visual variety. The bright colors will work even when baby is older, although she may wish to add another color to update the space.

TIMELESS ELEMENTS. Add a plethora of storage to ensure everything has a place—whether it's baby toys now or stacks of magazines later. The focal point of this room is a window seat flanked by bookcases custom-fit with cubbies of varied sizes that display treasured items.

A matching crib and twin bed ensure a cohesive look, although the transition to the bed is still a few years away. Underbed space is prime real estate, so shallow bins that roll under the box spring provide an extra spot for stashing belongings. Alternatively, the space could fit a trundle bed for sleepovers.

COOL CUBBIES

(LEFT) Books, toys, and felt blocks fill a wall of cubbies. The background of each cubby is painted a different color to add depth.

At the wondrous moment you were born, as you took your first breath, a great celebration was held in the heavens and twelve magnificent gifts were granted to you.

WRITE THIS
This hue-happy room includes a passage from a book handpainted above the bed.

TWO'S COMPANY (ABOVE) The crib is baby's sleeping place now; in a few years it can be removed and baby turned toddler can use the matching bed.

DRESSING UP (LEFT) A refurbished antique dresser serves as a changing table. Once baby grows, the pad can go and the dresser can stay in place.

EASY CHANGE (LEFT) This changing table easily transitioned to a stylish dresser once the changing pad was removed.

subtle shift

THE POWER OF PURPLE. The lavender walls of this bedroom set the backdrop for a space filled with splashy colors that will work from toddlerhood through adolescence. The blue, purple, and lime green colors painted on the wooden window valance are repeated throughout the room, creating a setting fit for an imaginative little girl or an energetic teen.

At this stage the room has been converted from a nursery to a child's room. The changing table was transformed into a dresser, and the cozy corner for rocking baby is now ideal for storytime. Bunkbeds replaced the crib; safety features—the ladder and railing— gain a touch of style with lavender paint. Removing the ladder and railing and separating the bunks into two twin beds will make the arrangement teen-friendly in a few years.

SWAPPING DETAILS. Choose a classic color scheme and traditional furniture to last. Then add details that ensure the room fits the age and tastes of its occupant. Here childhood memorabilia fills the custom-painted storage cubes above the dresser, fanciful paintings adorn the walls, and dolls dance above the chair in the reading corner. The items displayed on the walls are easily updated as tastes change, and even the bedding can be reversed if an older girl decides flowers aren't her style.

COOL CORNER (LEFT) The reading corner sets the tone with a funky upholstered ottoman, a scalloped lampshade that matches the wooden valance, and dolls suspended from the ceiling.

ON GUARD (ABOVE) Top bunks should include a sturdy guardrail that extends at least 5 inches above the mattress surface. This guardrail can be removed once it's time to separate the bunks into two twin beds.

easy transitions

Follow these decorating tips to make updating your child's room a cinch every step of the way.

▶ **BUY TRADITIONAL FURNITURE.** Furnishings with classic style appeal to young children as well as teens. Consider convertible pieces—a convertible crib may be transformed into a desk or chair, depending on the model. Furniture that's easy to move makes rearranging or moving to a bigger room easier.

▶ **GIVE YOUR CHILD OPTIONS.** A reversible comforter offers variety. If your child likes to hang stickers or artwork, add a corkboard to the wall so the decorations can be easily updated.

▶ **ADD PERSONALITY WITH ACCENTS.** Personalize with pillows, posters, and other changeable accents in your child's favorite color or theme.

PLAYFUL DETAILS

(RIGHT) Walls painted in a neutral but sunny hue are decorated with removable decals. The upholstered chair is for rocking now but is cool enough to stick around for years.

STINKY STATION (ABOVE) The changing pad on this dresser doubles as a fun play mat for the floor. Once baby outgrows diapers the dresser top serves as another spot for displaying decorative objects.

CLOSET STYLE (BELOW) A small walk-in closet provides a spot for everything from clothing to toys. A seat under a low window and French doors fitted with a punchy fabric add personality.

room to grow

KID-FRIENDLY. From a cozy crib along the wall to a built-in bed with a handy trundle beneath the window, this gender-neutral space has everything a child needs to sleep, play, and grow.

The supersaturated, high-contrast colors and patterns that fill the nursery introduce a baby's developing eyes to the wonders of his or her room; in later years those same hues will draw an energetic child to sprawl on the floor with toys or curl up on the bed with a book.

STAYING PUT. Select elements for the room that are designed to grow with the occupant. The crib is likely the exception. Here a variety of decorative, durable, and washable fabrics populate the space. A small walk-in closet, a trundle below the daybed, and tower shelving on each side of the window provide storage and display space.

STORE IT Built-in storage towers and inexpensive kitchen cabinets used as nightstands make the most of the space between the daybed and the wall.

bathrooms

Bathrooms are designed to be functional. If you add the right colors and accessories, they also can be fun. Even an ordinary bathroom can be transformed into a place for a splish-splashin' good time. Of course safety is important too—though your kids never need to know that those fun rugs and that funky stool serve a more practical purpose.

BY LAMPLIGHT (LEFT)
A sconce with two lamps provides extra brightness for teenage girls to apply makeup. The sconce design is basic, so it can adapt to future changes in decor.

MINOR CHANGES (ABOVE) Plain hardware was removed and replaced with seashell-shape knobs. Small, easy changes like this make it almost effortless to add fun twists to a child's bath.

PRACTICAL PLANS
With easily accessible light switches and electrical outlets, this is a convenient space. If younger children use the room, outlet covers can be added for safety.

double up on fun

FUNCTIONAL DESIGN. Bathrooms for children must be safe, storage-savvy, and easy to use. These features become even more important in a shared bath. Two teenage girls use this bright bathroom, which sits between their separate bedrooms. One bedroom is pink and the other is purple, so the bath color scheme needed to coordinate with both. Two-tone pink stripes on the walls fit the bill.

To accommodate both girls the vanity area features two sinks and a large mirror that takes up most of the wall. Undercounter cabinets and drawers provide space for keeping makeup and curling irons out of sight. If your bathroom is tight on storage space, consider an inexpensive set of plastic drawers or wall shelves that won't take up floor space.

PERSONALITY INFUSED. Most bathrooms are relatively small spaces, yet they can always accommodate extra personality. Use details to add character, such as the seashell-inspired drawer hardware pictured here. A coat of paint also works wonders. Here vertical stripes elongate the space while looking especially stylish.

children's bath accessories

Scrub-a-dub with fun, functional accessories made for the bath.

▶ **TOY STORAGE** is a must for keeping clutter to a minimum. Mesh bags with suction cups attach to shower walls and allow toys to drain into the tub.

▶ **STEP STOOLS** come in fun colors and designs and ensure that little ones can reach the sink. Look for stools that are light enough for toddlers to move yet sturdy enough to hold a child.

▶ **CUSHIONED FAUCET COVERS**—some even featuring animal designs—slip over the tub faucet to soften edges in case kids slip.

▶ **MINI SHOWER MATS OR TUB TREADS** come in a plethora of designs to fit a kid-friendly theme. They're fun to walk on and keep the tub safe.

LIGHTEN UP The metal shelving unit proves that even storage pieces can be decorative. Sheer cotton batiste fabric and cheery green ribbons add softness to the practical metal element.

FANCY FLIGHT

(RIGHT) Traced from a coloring book, this delicate butterfly adds a playful touch.

CASUAL MIX (LEFT)
A variety of fabrics combine in this eye-catching shower curtain, while a potted plant reinforces the garden theme.

garden variety

EVERYTHING IN ITS PLACE.
Bathrooms present an interesting contradiction: They're often the smallest room in a house, yet they have to store so much. Think creatively to keep your children's toiletries and towels organized. In addition to undercounter cabinets, this bath uses a row of wall hooks instead of a freestanding shelf to avoid crowding the vanity. Tall shelving—such as this metal unit—makes use of vertical space to keep odds and ends neat. The garden theme—with soft greens, butterfly details, and floral prints—adds a warm touch to the hardworking storage pieces.

FLOOR FACTORS. Tile or linoleum floors can be chilly and slippery for little feet. A fuzzy floor rug is a good solution; add slip-proof backing because loose rugs are a major tripping hazard.

BASIC BEAUTY

(LEFT) A cream-color countertop and rosy cabinetry make this vanity dazzling. The cheerful but not too childish colors will adapt to many themes.

COLOR CHOICES
(LEFT) In the girl's bedroom bright pink rules. In her bathroom, though, a more neutral yellow tone graces the walls, and pink appears in details such as the wall mural.

easy themes

KEEPING IT CONSISTENT. When a bathroom is connected to a child's room, creating one theme for both is a great way to unify the spaces. In the bath the theme can be subtle. These two baths incorporate just enough of their bedrooms' themes to get the point across—a practical approach if tastes change over the years.

The little girl's bath carries over flowers from the bedroom mural and features a similar color palette. Other than that the elements are kept basic. The vanity, mirror, and sconces are timeless, while black accents ground the space.

A sports-theme bathroom is a perfect extension of a boy's bedroom. Select basic tones for large elements in the bath, such as the deep red of this vanity and mirror frame. Details are used sparingly yet add personality to the space. For example, custom-made sports-motif cutouts surround the mirror, while sports-theme picture frames grace the countertop. These details are easy to change later on when the space becomes a guest bath.

GROWING UP
(LEFT) Black accessories keep the space from looking too young, while the shower curtain valance mimics the window treatments in the bedroom.

BOLD HUES (BELOW) A bright but basic red makes the vanity versatile in this boy's bath. For now it's a fun dose of color; later surrounding details may change so the hue looks more mature.

HOME FIELD ADVANTAGE (LEFT) Fun chalkboards play up the sports theme the bath and bedroom share. Later they can easily be removed from the wall.

bathroom
safety

Before kids splash around in the bath, make certain it's safe for get-clean fun.

▶ **SECURE LOWER CABINETS** and drawers using press-release latches, spring latches, or locks.

▶ **KEEP THE TOILET SEAT DOWN** with a toilet lid latch.

▶ **USE SLIP-RESISTANT MATERIALS** on the floor and traction strips in the tub.

▶ **KEEP MEDICINES** out of reach.

▶ **USE PLASTIC**—not glass—tumblers and other accessories.

▶ **INSTALL QUICK-ACCESS** privacy locks on doors so you can get in quickly.

▶ **PICK UP OBJECTS** left out, especially those small enough to swallow or that might cause little ones to fall.

▶ **KEEP CURLING IRONS,** hair dryers, and electric-blade razors out of reach.

bonus spaces

Playtime can extend beyond your child's bedroom if you create a designated toy room or crafts space in your home. Consider the activities your child is likely to undertake—from building with blocks to playing dress-up to painting—and plan accordingly. Remember, they're called playrooms for a reason, so feel free to have a bit of fun with the decor.

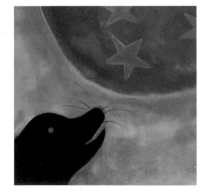

CANVAS CARRIER
(RIGHT) Canvas shoe bags, typically used behind closet doors, are perfect for storing pens, pencils, small brushes, rulers, and sketch pads.

family crafts

SETTING THE SCENE. If you have artistic kids in the house, an efficient and inspiring crafts room is one way to provide a venue for fostering creativity and organizing art supplies. Fancy decor is unnecessary in this family-approved art space, where cheery green paint and little else cover the walls. Instead the walls and even the windows are adorned with smart tools for organizing everything budding artists need.

ALL IN PLACE. On one wall a clear plastic pocket organizer (not shown) keeps paints and other supplies visible. Nearby canvas shoe bags hang from the windows on drapery rings and clips, storing everything from colored pencils to swatches of paper. Adjustable shelves hang above the desk on one wall and above portable drawers that double as a gift-wrapping center on another. Glass containers and cans with colorful labels corral small items. Near the desk a low combination stool and magazine rack with a small plastic chair provides a spot for little ones to color.

CATCHALL CARTS
(RIGHT) A customized stack of mesh drawers serves as crafts central. The drawers keep supplies contained yet visible, while the tops of the carts provide additional workspace.

ALL SET (ABOVE) A 5-foot-long desk offers plenty of room for spreading out projects or opening scrapbooks flat. The adjustable desk chair allows parents or kids to work comfortably. Above the desk a shelf system organizes supplies.

clutter control

Bonus spaces such as crafts and toy rooms are particularly susceptible to clutter. Consider these ideas for keeping things tidy.

- ▶ **STASH SMALL ITEMS** in interesting, easily accessible containers such as hardware bins, spice jars, or even metal lunch boxes.

- ▶ **INVEST IN ROLLING CARTS** for maximum flexibility. If kids squabble over toys or supplies, dedicate one cart to each family member.

- ▶ **PROVIDE STORAGE OPTIONS** for little ones by placing pullout baskets or drawers low to the ground. Use picture labels to help tots put items back in the right spot.

- ▶ **GET CREATIVE** with containers that match the design theme—for instance, bright rain boots are a fun option for corralling supplies in a room with rainy-day decor.

- ▶ **CONSIDER HANGING** items to clear up more floor or desk space. Rods with curtain clips or a clothesline and clothespins provide options for clutter control and display.

DISAPPEARING ACT

(LEFT) A wall of built-in cabinetry keeps toys, games, and dress-up clothes out of view while doubling as an entertainment center. The citrus hues on the cabinets are found throughout the room.

TABLE SERVICE

(LEFT) Situated on a platform in front of an expanse of windows, a table provides a spot for crafts projects and tea parties. When children are older it will serve as space for homework.

fun & funky

DOUBLE DUTY. Rather than reserving an entire room for kids' play, create a multifunctional space. This large room combines the fun of a play area with the convenience of a guest room. The two twin beds that form an L-shape sofa in one corner can be pulled apart for overnight guests. Other elements in the room—such as a cozy seating area, a built-in entertainment center, and full-size table and chairs located near a bank of windows—can be used by adults as well as children.

To put everyone in a playful mood, decorate with fun in mind. Here the citrus-hue space bedecked in bold patterns and colorful shapes is bound to inspire play. The handpainted cabinets store toys and games, and a raised floor at the crafts end of the room doubles as a stage for kids' performances.

**BLACK & WHITE
& FUN ALL OVER**
Easy-care carpet tiles
combined with bright
yet simple fabrics are
a recipe for fun rather
than fussing in this
multifunctional room.

SPACE TO PLAY This playroom appears bright and open thanks to cheerful colors and big windows. White wainscoting and trim keep the look clean and classic, while the chairs and accessories add color.

GET CREATIVE

(RIGHT) An art table gives kids space to spread out their work. Above the wainscoting, chalkboard paint is a fun idea. A molding ledge doubles as a tray for chalk.

CLASSIC TWIST

(LEFT) A vintage school desk is painted to coordinate with the soft primary colors throughout the room.

a bit of everything

SIMPLE FUN. A playroom can be as fanciful or as basic as you like. This room takes the basic approach, which is a wise choice if the space will take on a new function once children grow older. White wainscoting looks classic and adds architectural interest. It's also durable and easy to clean if art projects stray from the table. Chalkboard paint creates a border above the wainscoting—a perfect height for children to doodle.

Storage is key for keeping a playroom neat and tidy. This room benefits from an entire wall of built-in shelves and cabinets, which keep games and art supplies organized. If you need to add storage items, plastic bins, wicker baskets, and tall bookcases are all handy and inexpensive solutions.

Soft primary colors enhance the classic appeal of the room. Cheery yellow-painted built-ins and sky blue walls set the lighthearted tone. The table set was purchased from an unpainted furniture store and painted different colors to brighten the space. A large rug in the center of the room adds warmth to the hardwood floor, making it more inviting for kids who want to sprawl out and play with toys.

COZY CORNER

(ABOVE) A child-size chair and ottoman add a grown-up look to the space. A funky lamp ensures that kids will have plenty of light when they curl up with a few books.

GET TO WORK (ABOVE) White-painted desks sit side by side along one wall, providing a spot for each child to tackle homework or play on the computer.

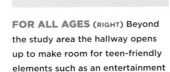

FOR ALL AGES (RIGHT) Beyond the study area the hallway opens up to make room for teen-friendly elements such as an entertainment center hidden in a white armoire and a comfortable sofa.

HOP AROUND (LEFT)
A painted hopscotch board and racetrack make the narrow stretch of floor near the stairs perfect for a child's playtime.

hallway play

CREATIVE USE. If a handful of kids live under one roof, space is probably at a premium. Carving out room for play and homework for kids ranging in age from 3 to 13 takes some ingenuity. In this home a large upstairs hallway that leads to the children's bedrooms serves as a communal study area and playroom complete with an entertainment area, desks, and storage.

COLOR CUES. Color rules in this hallway play zone: Painted octagons appear on the walls; a cloudy blue sky decorates the ceiling; and a racetrack, hopscotch board, and checkerboard liven up the hardwood floor. The happy hues of the chairs, red couch, and colorful storage bins on the shelves add to the energy of the space. White-painted furnishings that match the doors and trimwork balance the color scheme and keep the space from feeling too busy.

BEAUTIFUL BUILT-INS

(ABOVE) Built-ins provide an easy way to pack function into a small space. This wall features an entertainment center flanked by desks and shelving.

READY FOR THE KIDS

(LEFT) Placing a crafts table near a window ensures kids have plenty of light for projects. This pint-size setup can be removed when little ones outgrow it.

ENERGETIC ACCENTS (RIGHT)
Colorful paintings, an ottoman upholstered in yellow and red leather, and matching paper shades on the chandelier add color and energy to a room painted in a neutral hue.

made to last

LOOK TO THE FUTURE. Someday your little ones will grow. They require a toddler-friendly space now; yet in a very short time, they'll want a super cool place that's made for hanging out. To ease the transition consider outfitting a bonus space with durable, timeless elements such as the soft carpeting, denim upholstered seating, and white-painted storage found in this room. If you stick with basic pieces, you'll have a spot made for easy living, where spills are no big deal and creativity thrives.

For now the ottoman and built-in shelving store toys and children's books; the furnishings include a kid-size table and small yellow and red upholstered chairs. In a few years the desks on either side of the entertainment center can accommodate older kids doing homework, and the couches will be ideal for seating friends during movie time.

BRIGHT LIGHT (BELOW) The linen Roman window shades filter some sunlight while keeping the room light and airy.

paint

One of the easiest ways to add personality to a room, paint is a must-have for children's spaces. Make a statement with bold hues, big stripes, or detailed murals. And remember that paint works on furniture as well as walls; apply a coat or two to furnishings for an instant update. Is your child tired of the current color scheme? Lucky you. Paint is easy to change on a whim.

 **MAKING WAVES**

(ABOVE) Murals come
in all shapes and sizes,
as this nautical-theme
room demonstrates. A
small design resembling
an island-view porthole
is eye-catching against
the neutral walls.

RAISE THE FLAG

(RIGHT) A bookcase with
a flag backdrop serves
as a patriotic resting
spot for belongings.
The neutral wall colors
behind it keep this
bold accent from
overwhelming the eye.

EARTHY SCENE
(LEFT) Touches of turquoise and lime green punch up a warm, natural color scheme in a gender-neutral nursery.

color basics

HUE-HAPPY. The easiest way to infuse a child's room with personality—whether it's a soothing space for sweet dreams or a retreat for fun-filled afternoons—is through paint. Before you begin splashing color on the walls, it pays to consider the basics. The primary colors—red, blue, and yellow—are the three basic colors from which all other colors are mixed. Secondary colors are created by mixing two primary colors; tertiary colors are made by combining a primary and a secondary color.

SPIN THE WHEEL. The color wheel is a useful tool for choosing color combinations. Colors next to each other on the color wheel (such as blue and green) are called analogous. Opposites (such as orange and blue) are complementary, and when used together each makes the other appear brighter and more intense. A monochromatic scheme combines a single color with a neutral (such as red with white). Finally, a triadic color scheme incorporates three colors, each evenly spaced from the others on the color wheel (try red, yellow, and blue).

YUMMY COMBO
(RIGHT) Complementary colors such as pale blue (a cool tone) and chocolate brown (a warm tone) work well together because they play off of one another.

FOLLOW THE RAINBOW (LEFT)
A rainbow of bold random-width vertical stripes on the wall provides plenty of opportunity for playing with color combinations in this bright teen room.

color schemes

SUPER SHADES. If you would rather not repaint the entire room every time your child's tastes change, select timeless hues that work with a variety of decorating schemes. However, if you consider paint a low-risk, low-commitment way to infuse a room with color, go for the bold trendy shades or decorative painting your child wants. If you want to paint over it later, maybe your child can help.

COLOR DILEMMA. If you need inspiration for a color scheme, look around. Favorite colors, fabrics, art, objects, or even storybook characters (either yours or your child's) may provide a starting point. Once you have selected a favorite color or two, your work begins in earnest: The goal is to find the right combination of shades, tints, and tones and to balance warm and cool colors so the room appears welcoming. Color can be used to manipulate the way the eye perceives a space too: Warm, or advancing, colors make a space appear smaller and cozier, while cool, or receding, colors create the appearance of a larger, airier room.

BLACK IS BACK
(LEFT) Black walls in a washable flat paint are the backdrop for a creative tween room. Light-color accents on the bed keep the room from feeling gloomy.

STRIPES RULE

(ABOVE) The striped fabric of the Roman shades inspired this red, navy, white, and green color scheme. A painted band of matching stripes on the deep blue walls furthers the look.

color trends

Some color schemes have staying power; others change as quickly as children grow. Try these trends on for size.

▶ **SPLASHING BRIGHT HUES** such as lime green and orange on walls can create a great look. If an entirely orange room seems overwhelming, go neutral on the walls and select bright-color accents such as pillows and lampshades to accessorize the room instead.

▶ **SELECTING TIMELESS COMBINATIONS** such as red, blue, and khaki offers plenty of opportunity for playful kids' spaces that easily transition to grown-up rooms.

▶ **PAIRING PINK** with purple or lime green is a big hit with little princesses.

▶ **ADDING BROWN**—particularly chocolate, mocha, and toffee—creates a delicious color scheme. Pair brown with cool blue for particularly striking results.

ALL ABOARD (ABOVE)
Professional painters created this mural of steam locomotives. Painting some areas of the mural in lighter hues prevents the walls from overpowering the room.

LOOK UP (RIGHT) White-painted molding separates chartreuse walls from a blue-painted ceiling that mimics the sky. Ceiling paint is specially formulated to diffuse light from lamps, windows, and other sources of illumination and offers better spatter resistance for overhead rolling than wall paint.

ANIMAL FUN (LEFT)
Cuddly-looking jungle
animals suit a boy's nursery.
A similar look can be
achieved by sponge painting
or stenciling and stippling.

techniques & ideas

GO FOR GLOSS. Although it may cost
a bit more, high-quality paint produced
by a well-known manufacturer is a
wise investment. In general such paint
requires fewer coats and lasts longer.
Look for semigloss or eggshell paints,
which are good at resisting stains and
are easier to clean than flat finishes.
Purchase enough paint to finish the
job—a gallon of paint should cover 400
to 450 square feet. Turn to page 142 for
more painting tips.

ENDLESS CHOICES. Painting solid-
color walls is an easy way to add
personality to a room. Or consider the
possibilities of decorative painting
techniques, from stripes or blocks of
color to stenciled shapes or freehand
drawings. You may wish to hire a
professional to paint a mural on your
child's wall. Or consider painting a
portion of a wall with chalkboard paint
so your child has a place to draw, write,
and display artwork. Remember too that
ceilings, floors, and even furnishings may
benefit from a couple of coats of paint.

DECORATIVE TOUCH
(ABOVE) This armoire,
desk, and bed boast
detailed designs that were
handpainted by an artist.
Whether done with stencils
or by a local artist, creatively
painted furniture gives any
room a one-of-a-kind look.

SAIL AWAY (LEFT)
Custom-cut stencils were used to create the sailboat shapes and roping on the walls in a nautical-theme room.

FLOOR MODEL (RIGHT) This newly installed wide-plank pine floor was aged and painted to look like green gingham fabric. The floor was sealed to protect the paint.

IN THE DETAILS (BELOW) The inset panels of this built-in sport a vibrant pink paint to match the geometric-print Roman shade that covers the bookshelves above.

professional
painting tips

Follow these pointers for a stellar paint job.

▶ **PREPARE** the walls by sealing any cracks and gaps around windows and baseboards with a water-base, paintable caulk. Repair nail holes too.

▶ **LINE** baseboards, trim, and ceilings with low-tack adhesive masking tape.

▶ **REMOVE** furnishings and accessories. Lay a canvas drop cloth on the floor. Remove all fixture covers too.

▶ **SELECT** a quality brush and roller that are appropriate for the painting job at hand—your local Home Depot can help.

▶ **PRIME** the wall before painting, unless the old paint is clean and adhering well.

▶ **PAINT** the moldings closest to the ceiling first and work your way down.

ROUND 'EM UP Large bright pink and orange circles on light pink walls spice up this little girl's room. The painted circles mimic the round shapes on the bedding.

fabrics

From comfortable cotton bedding to warm, fuzzy pillow covers, a variety of fabrics appeal to children of all ages. Patterns are popular too. Whether in window treatments or colorful upholstery, they energize kids' rooms. The secret to using fabrics well lies in finding the right mix of textures, colors, and patterns. Beyond that it's all about personal tastes.

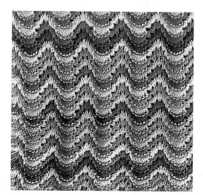

STELLAR STYLE

(RIGHT) Planets float on pillows and window coverings in this boy's room. Patterned fabrics make it easy to create a theme with accents such as window treatments and bedspreads.

HIGH IMPACT (LEFT)
This expensive fabric covers an ottoman rather than an entire chair. Limiting its use contained fabric costs and introduced a small dose of jazzy pattern.

FROG-WORTHY

(LEFT) In cool blue and grassy green, the simple stripes and zigzags of this bedding are made for longevity. The hues found in the fabrics are repeated on the wall and display cubes.

fabric basics

FABRIC TYPES. Different parts of a room may require different fabric types. To determine which fabrics work best for your child's room, think function first. Perhaps the top choice for kids' rooms, tight-weave cotton or cotton blends (such as cotton and polyester) make long-wearing, washable options for seating, bedding, and drapery fabrics.

TEXTURE & PATTERN. Children enjoy texture, so fabrics with varied surfaces, such as a nubby cotton blanket, soft flannel sheets, or a cuddly chenille throw, may make kids' spaces more inviting. Mixing fabric patterns and colors ensures visual interest. The key is to begin with one print you love; then work in color-related fabrics to complement it. (See "Mixing Patterns" on page 103 for more information.) Remember to bring home samples of fabrics to see how they look before making final selections.

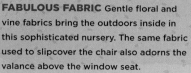

FABULOUS FABRIC Gentle floral and vine fabrics bring the outdoors inside in this sophisticated nursery. The same fabric used to slipcover the chair also adorns the valance above the window seat.

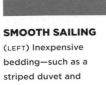

SMOOTH SAILING
(LEFT) Inexpensive bedding—such as a striped duvet and pirate-theme pillow—enhances a nautical-theme boy's room.

bedding

EASY USE. In a child's room (or any bedroom for that matter), the bed is the place where fabric rules. Though options for materials, colors, and patterns are limited only by your imagination or budget, a few guidelines may help you when selecting linens. In general stay away from expensive fabrics that must be hand-washed or dry-cleaned. If you have a gorgeous length of silk, however, consider having it made into a bedskirt or a window treatment—two places where fabric is less likely to suffer stains or wear.

PERFECT COMBOS. Bed-in-a-bag kits are one inexpensive and easy option for outfitting a bed in coordinating fabrics. Or select reversible linens that give your child style options. For a long-lasting look choose quality solid-color fabrics and add splashes of color and pattern with throw pillows. Then again you may wish to use sheets or a comforter (or both) as an inexpensive means of showcasing your child's interests. Once your child outgrows a theme, simply swap out the thematic elements for something new.

BE PREPARED (BELOW) Although it's hidden from sight beneath a washable bedspread, this toddler-ready mattress is covered in a waterproof mattress protector and durable bedding.

LUXE STYLE (ABOVE)
Luxurious fabrics—including silk, cotton, and linen—abound on a fabric-covered headboard, multilayered corona, duvet cover, bedskirt, and bolster.

TOTALLY MOD (LEFT) This teen bed is piled high with pillows covered in bright, patterned cotton. The fuzzy white pillow adds textural variety to the mix.

SWEET VINTAGE (ABOVE) Fabrics needn't be childlike to fit in a kid's room. A patchwork quilt of vintage fabric is the highlight of the linens layered on this pretty, feminine bed.

DO DOTS (LEFT)
Coordinate bedding with other fabrics for a cohesive color scheme. Here reversed patterns on the bedskirt and curtains match without overwhelming the room.

PATCHWORK (RIGHT)
This bedding was made of squares of chenille pieced together like a patchwork quilt. Tiny decorative pillows made from luxe fabrics add color and texture.

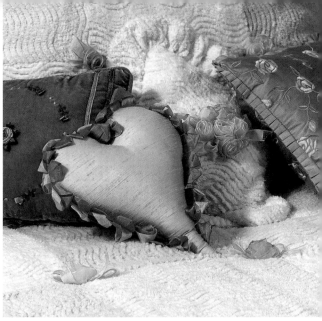

CLASSIC VARIETY Bedding and pillows in this nautical room mix different-size stripes. The result is clean and classic, as well as visually interesting.

allergy-free
rooms

Even children with allergies can have fabulous fabric-filled bedrooms.

Reduce a dust-sensitive child's allergy troubles by sticking to natural-fiber bedding such as cotton, which holds less dust than synthetic materials. Hypoallergenic materials are becoming more comfortable—in fact, more companies are producing pillows and duvets filled with clean, natural hypoallergenic fills as soft as down. After carefully choosing your fabric, cover the mattress with an airtight, washable plastic cover or fit the frame with an air-filled mattress. Use low-VOC (volatile organic compound) paint on walls and purchase furnishings constructed of natural materials such as wood or cork to further reduce allergy problems.

textile ideas

MULTIPLE FUNCTIONS. Fabrics can be more than bedding and window treatments. Affix fabric to walls or even ceilings for a low-commitment alternative to painting. Cover a piece of plywood in batting and then wrap it with a favorite cloth to make an inexpensive headboard. Drape gauzy fabric above the bed as a canopy. Even storage items look more stylish with the addition of fabric: Line baskets, cover boxes, or create a curtain to hide clutter on shelves. Slipcovering furniture such as chairs in sturdy textiles makes sense for children's rooms too. When spills occur the slipcovers are easily removed and washed without damaging the chair upholstery.

FABRIC INSPIRATION. Think of fabrics as more than mere decorative elements. A hue from a favorite fabric might inspire a color scheme in your child's room. Fabrics may influence furnishing choices as well. If you select a favorite bedspread before purchasing a bed, a dark-color fabric may lead you to buy a bed with a lighter wood tone, or vice versa.

MADE FOR BABY (BELOW) Color and texture abound in this nursery, which includes an upholstered rocking chair in a nubby green fabric and an ottoman with pockets for tucking in favorite toys. A fabric-covered basket slides under the crib for hidden storage.

COLORFUL CLOSET (ABOVE) A flower-power curtain adds a burst of color to a closet and provides an easy means for hiding clutter. A fuzzy purple cover stands out on the butterfly chair.

window treatments

Want to lighten or brighten your child's room in a matter of minutes? Look to the windows. Beyond the natural light windows provide, they offer the perfect spot for furthering your decorating scheme. Plus shades, blinds, or curtains are ideal for blocking out light at naptime and providing privacy anytime.

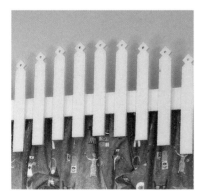

HOPPING ALONG
(LEFT) The bunny-print fabric on the cornice and draperies launched a kicky design scheme. The green and white checked shade blocks light when it's time for a nap.

window treatment basics

PRETTY DETAILS
(LEFT) Silk rosettes from a crafts-supply store were coated with shellac for stiffness and mounted at the top of these golden full-length silk draperies embroidered with roses.

STYLE CHOICES. Window treatments serve three main functions: regulating the amount of light entering a room, providing privacy, and enhancing the style of the room. Valances and cornices are decorative curtains or bands, respectively, used to conceal the mounting hardware at the top of curtain fixtures. Shades and blinds are practical, fitted treatments for blocking light and views. Draperies and curtains are other decorative options for obtaining privacy and light control. A window treatment that combines shades, draperies, and a valance might become the focal point of a room. In children's rooms, however, simple is best, so a single window treatment may suffice.

SAFETY & FUNCTION. The first step in selecting window treatments is to consider safety. For specifics see "Window Treatment Safety" on page 161. Then contemplate function. Keep light out for naptime or bedtime by using blinds or soft fabric shades with blackout linings. Outside-mount shades provide better light protection than inside-mount ones. Once you have chosen a basic style, look at fabrics and decorative touches.

EASY-OPEN (LEFT) White-painted shutters can be opened to let in sunlight. They're a simple alternative to blinds or shades in a child's room.

SEAWORTHY Boating rope looped through metal grommets lends a finishing touch to the striped window shades. Blinds add an extra layer of privacy and light control behind the Roman shades.

FLOWERY FUN This flower-print window treatment lowers for privacy. The strands of ribbon that hang down aren't safe for a young child's room but add a decorative touch in a teen space.

SPACE-AGE (ABOVE) This space-inspired roller shade was decorated by stamping paint-dipped household items such as measuring cups and plastic lids on the fabric. The sheer polka-dot curtains further the theme.

SWEET TOPPING (ABOVE) Pickets on these cornices enhance a garden theme. Balloon shades soften the vertical lines of the valance and add a playful touch.

techniques
& ideas

WINDOW SAVVY. Consider whether you want window treatments with staying power or ones that match your child's current tastes. Higher-priced fabrics may offer the quality suited for longevity. Or select cellular shades or wood blinds, which control light and provide a clean look regardless of the decorating scheme.

Window treatments are a great way to enhance a theme, however, because you can repeat fabrics used elsewhere. Add interesting details—a contrasting border, welted edges, or ribbon ties—to enhance an otherwise ho-hum window treatment. And remember that layering—combining, say, a painted roller shade with a checked valance or sheer curtains—is an easy way to add visual interest.

INDOOR-OUTDOOR (LEFT) An outdoor-inspired awning goes girly with a floral scallop border. Interior awnings break up a boxy room and add depth and angular interest.

TWICE AS NICE A Roman shade blocks light, while a vibrant balloon shade is more decorative. Using a double or triple window treatment is one way to make windows a focal point.

SAIL AWAY (LEFT) Tiebacks can be more than functional. Handmade sailboat holdbacks and ticking tiebacks bring seafaring style to simple white curtains in an ocean-inspired room.

LANTERN LOOK

(RIGHT) Blue and white striped lanterns serve as a unique valance and hide the mechanics of sun-blocking roller shades. The little bows add a feminine touch.

SHADY SPOT (BELOW) Minimal window treatments do the trick in a busy room. Here shades can be lowered to block light, while a fanciful giant leaf provides shade over a toddler bed.

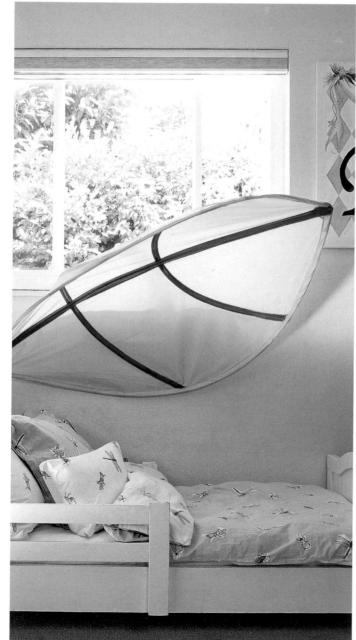

window
treatment
safety

Think safety first when selecting window treatments.

Blinds and other window hangings—particularly those with cords—may pose a risk to children. Eliminate the risk by moving cribs, beds, and other furniture away from windows. Safety guidelines require that blinds made before 2001 be replaced or retrofitted with cord stops, tassels, or tie-down devices. Cordless blinds, shades, and draperies are the safest alternatives to cord-operated products. Options include cordless horizontal and vertical blinds, pleated shades, fabric roll-up shades, and wood blinds operated with a remote control. Newer systems provide even more versatility: Cellular shades feature spring-loaded mechanisms that require only a push or pull in the center of the bottom rail handle to raise or lower the shades.

furnishings

Without furnishings a room is only an empty box. In a child's bedroom the most important piece of furniture is, of course, the bed. Beyond that the basics vary with age: Little ones require a changing table, toddlers need toy storage, and older kids will want a desk for doing homework. Include accessories too. Well-placed rugs, lighting, and artwork help complete the room.

SMART DESIGN

(LEFT) Modern cribs are known for melding style and function. In this case a changing table clips on the crib. Once baby grows the crib converts to a toddler bed.

MOVABLE MATTRESS

(ABOVE) A crib with an adjustable mattress is best because the mattress can be lowered once baby is big enough to stand in the crib. A child more than a few inches taller than the crib rails should be moved to a toddler bed.

cribs

THINK SAFETY. The crib is the most important element in a nursery because babies require a safe, comfortable place to sleep. Although a cradle or bassinet may work for newborns, your baby will use a crib for two or three years, so make certain you purchase a stable, quality one with a firm, tight-fitting mattress.

Any crib you purchase—whether new or used—should include a certification seal showing that it meets national safety standards. Make certain the slats are not more than $2\frac{3}{8}$ inches apart. Decorative cutouts on the headboard or footboard are another no-no because a baby's head could get caught.

BABY STYLE. Although safety is a top priority for crib selection, consider style as well. Natural wood or neutral-color cribs work well with a variety of bedding. For a personalized touch decorate your little one's crib with lead-free paint.

MADE TO MATCH With built-in storage below and shelves above, this painted changing table complements the room's red decorating scheme.

THE RIGHT HEIGHT (RIGHT) A changing table should be waist-height for comfort. Hanging often-used items above the table keeps bending to a minimum—but the items must be well out of baby's reach.

NICE VIEW (ABOVE) A fanciful mural adorns the wall above this table, providing a welcome distraction for baby. Fabric-lined baskets below ensure items such as diapers are easy to reach.

EASY OPTION (LEFT) A standard dresser works as a changing table when outfitted with a changing pad that has raised sides to help keep baby in place.

changing tables

READY FOR USE. Changing diapers will be a regular daily—or even hourly—occurrence for the first couple of years of your baby's life. To make the process of changing diapers comfortable and safe for you and your child, include a changing table in the nursery floor plan.

A changing table may be a piece of furniture expressly made for that function, complete with easily accessible drawers or shelves underneath for storing necessities. A changing table can also be as simple as a dresser or a countertop, as long as it's sturdy and includes a changing pad and safety features to help prevent baby from falling.

QUICK CHANGE

(LEFT) Who would guess a kitchen island could double as a changing table? The height is just right, and this one offers ample storage. The casters lock in place or allow the table to be moved.

STOWAWAY Decorative fronts and pulls on the trundle of this bed allude to what hides within—neatly stored toys and extra bedding.

TRUNDLE FOR TWO
A twin-size trundle bed is a space-saving, safe solution for accommodating guests during sleepovers.

beds

BIG BUNKS (BELOW) Basic pieces such as a hardwood full-size bed under a twin bunk remain useful even as children grow. As tastes change, so can the bedding.

SWEET DREAMS. Once a child is big enough to climb out of the crib, it's time to move on to a big-kid bed. To ease the transition your child may benefit from a toddler bed (see "A Bed that Grows with Baby," page 170). Many toddlers easily move from a crib to a twin-size bed. Bunkbeds are popular among youngsters and are a space-saving option—particularly if siblings share a room. Think safety with lofted beds; check for weight recommendations, bed sturdiness, and features such as railings. Although twin beds work best for young children, tweens and teens may prefer a full-size setup.

BEST BETS. Look for furniture that can adapt to your child's age. Novelty beds are fun at first, but children's tastes change. It's easier and less expensive to create a theme with paint, fabric, and bedding. Purchase a quality bed, and regardless of style—traditional, four-poster, or even platform—it's bound to last.

DOUBLE TAKE (ABOVE) When two twin beds must fit in a small room, arranging them against the walls preserves enough floor space for fun.

MADE TO LAST (ABOVE) A full-size bed with a black headboard fits most decorating schemes. Niches in the headboard allow for a changing display of accessories.

a bed that **grows with baby**

Save yourself the trouble of purchasing a new bed as your baby grows by buying a convertible crib that easily changes into a toddler bed or daybed and beyond.

Purchasing a convertible crib saves you the hassle of buying a new bed as soon as your baby outgrows the crib. Convertible cribs may be more expensive, but they're often a worthwhile investment. Converting a crib to a toddler's bed takes up less space than replacing it with a twin-size bed, plus toddler beds sit lower to the ground and may include rails for safety. Some models convert from a crib to a fashionable daybed simply by dropping a single rail. And many models now go beyond these basic conversions. Some transition from crib to bed to furnishings such as chairs; others move from crib to toddler bed to a full-size model with minimal effort. Purchase a bed constructed from quality materials so it will last for years.

ON FIRE (ABOVE) The fireman theme in this room is evident in the bed frame shaped like a fire engine. Rather than a headboard, a wall mural of a firehouse distinguishes the sleeping area.

SIT HERE (ABOVE) Even small spaces can offer several seating options. This room includes matching upholstered chairs for parent and child, a window seat, and a stool.

SITTING PRETTY

(RIGHT) A white wicker glider and ottoman provide the perfect spot for rocking baby. The cushions are upholstered in the same fabric as the one on the adjacent window seat.

seating

MADE FOR TWO. Children's rooms are used for more than sleeping; they're also havens for rocking little ones to sleep, sharing stories, and relaxing. Select seating that comfortably accommodates parents and children and that fits the style of the room.

A cozy chair such as a rocker or glider is ideal for feeding or soothing a baby. Chairs upholstered in durable, stain-resistant fabrics are best at withstanding wear. Regardless of style chairs should be sturdy. Kid-size seats provide a comfortable spot for little ones to read or play on their own. Or select a comfortable chair and ottoman that will work in your child's room now and in a different part of the house later.

WINDOW SEATS. Plan a built-in bench in front of a window to include seating in a child's room, particularly if floor space is tight. A soft cushion will welcome kids and provide a spot to sprawl out, gaze out the window, or take a nap. Upholster the cushion in fabric that fits with the current decorating scheme; it can always be changed later.

IN THE FUN SEAT

(RIGHT) A funky hanging chair fits perfectly in a tween girl's room. Such a large piece should be securely attached to the ceiling beams.

work surfaces

WOBBLE-FREE. You've heard it before
yet it's worth repeating: Furnishings in
children's spaces must be sturdy. This
is particularly true with work surfaces,
which should endure the weight of
children who lean across the crafts
table to grab a crayon or the thump of
schoolbooks hefted onto the corner of
a teen's desk. Of course, durability is
important too. Look for surfaces that can
be wiped clean of spills and that endure
marks from writing instruments.

WORKABLE OPTIONS. In youngsters'
spaces a child-size table and chairs are
a good bet. As children get older they'll
probably benefit from a desk with a
comfortable chair. Make certain the desk
and chair heights are appropriate for
your child's size. The placement of a desk
matters too. If possible position the desk
near electrical outlets for plugging in
lighting and a computer.

MADE TO GROW

(LEFT) This little-girl work area can grow with the girl. The versatile modular cubes on the desk can be used to raise the desk height. Then all that's needed is a bigger chair.

READY FOR ACTION

(LEFT) A pint-size easy-to-clean table and matching chairs provide a spot for a toddler and his friends to play. Toys and art supplies are stored in plastic bins in the small bench.

UNDER THE STAIRS In children's rooms even nooks and crannies such as this spot (under stairs leading to a play space) are perfect for storage. Built-in bookcases that display a child's playthings next to the bed are a parent's dream, as long as the child knows not to climb on them.

FIGHTING FADS
(RIGHT) A classic wood dresser with red accents may stay in the room even after the child outgrows his interest in firefighters.

ALL FOR ME (BELOW) Glass jars, metal clipboards, fiber baskets, and wood cubbies allow older children to arrange and display treasures on their own.

storage

EVERYTHING IN ITS PLACE. Children's rooms require more than the bureau and closet typically found in grown-up spaces. Storage must be practical, yet it can still be fun. With the right combination of pieces, all of a child's belongings can be stashed stylishly and still be accessible when it's time for play.

SMART STOWAWAY. Think first about the objects that occupy your child's space. Building blocks and toy cars require different containers than books, collectibles, and CDs. Beware of heavy toy chests that can pinch fingers. Lightweight drawers are better; or fill the room with sturdy open shelving (see "Outside the Toy Box" on page 179). Underbed space is prime real estate where shallow bins with wheels can hide items out of sight. Other options, such as lockers, built-in storage benches, and collapsible tubs, ensure that everything has its place.

DRESSING UP PRACTICAL (BELOW) A large bookshelf comfortably holds books, toys, and decorative pieces. The unit is designed to resemble a dollhouse, which adds a clever twist to a basic piece and makes keeping things organized a little more fun.

CLASSIC COUNTERPART (ABOVE) A traditional white armoire is a calm and classic element in a room filled with pink. Drawers, cabinets, and open shelving ensure practical and decorative objects have a place.

STORAGE SEATING (ABOVE)
Built-in window seat drawers maximize storage space in this girl's room. The drawers are a nice way to keep odds and ends out of sight.

TOO COOL (ABOVE)
This sleek, funky wall system doubles as an oversize headboard. The shelf unit bracketed directly to the wall sits on a separate base unit, creating a seamless integration with the bed.

outside the **toy box**

Have some fun with these creative storage solutions that keep shelving—whether open or hidden in cabinets—neat and tidy.

Shelving is great for stashing children's belongings, but without the proper organizational elements, items on shelves may fall into disarray. Get kids involved in the cleanup process by allowing them to decorate boxes or wooden crates to place on the shelves. Other stylish options include colorful plastic bins or baskets lined with fabric. Move beyond the standard storage containers and consider how tin pails, glass or plastic jars, and even old lunch boxes can function as fun storage for kids' spaces.

MARCHING ORDERS (LEFT) A scrap of fabric adorned with soldiers was hot-glued to a red place mat to create low-cost artwork. The old-style lampshade furthers the design.

BRIGHT IDEA (BELOW) This sitting area boasts serious personality thanks to a funky pendent light, fun pillows, and an end table with decorative details that match the color scheme.

accents

IN THE DETAILS. After the furnishings are in place, it's time to turn to the details. Decorative accents—whether they hang from the ceiling, adorn the walls, or rest on a dresser—ensure your child's room has distinctive personality and style. First select functional accents that further the decorating scheme: An area rug helps define a lounging zone or play space, a funky lamp provides light, and hooks on the wall create a spot for additional storage and display.

HAVE FUN. Once the basic decorative elements are established, it's time to play. Add a dose of reality to a theme room with accessories. For instance, rolling pins and baking sheets add authenticity to the bakeshop room on pages 56–57, while bobbers and nets would enhance a fishing theme. Hang artwork on the walls, add throw pillows to a window seat, or place framed photos on a nightstand for instant style. The addition of knickknacks, collectibles, or accents such as painted drawer knobs gives final polish to any room. Remember, though, small or breakable items should be displayed out of the reach of young ones.

SURFER DUDE

Surf icons rule in this room, which includes a handpainted bamboo curtain that matches the framed wall clock. A miniature surfboard and other items adorned with hibiscus blooms extend the theme.

CAMPOUT (ABOVE)
Fold-up camping cots, a picnic table, and Adirondack chairs define this play space. Beachy-keen wallpapers and rugs pair with an umbrella, an awning window treatment, and shutters for a summer-camp look.

FAR OUT (RIGHT) For easy accents in this space-theme room, out-of-this-world felt shapes adorn the pillows, and a child's outer-space paintings are displayed on the wall.

HANDY DISPLAY (RIGHT) It's easy to choose the jewelry for the day in this young girl's room. Instead of being hidden away and tangled in jewelry boxes, the necklaces are neatly hung on a brightly painted set of wall hooks.

READY FOR PLAY (ABOVE) In a baby's room a chunky rug is soft on the hands, knees, and feet. The animals that march along the perimeter enhance the zoo theme.

PRETTY PURPLES (ABOVE) A bright pink telephone on the desk and purple fabric covering the chair fill a teen girl's bedroom with energy.

accessory safety

In every child's room make certain that accessories are safe for little ones or are placed well out of reach.

The easiest way to ensure the accessories added to your child's room are safe is to examine each item before purchasing it. Safety is particularly important around cribs. Make sure mobiles and other hanging toys are higher than baby can reach and remove all decorative pillows and other items from the crib before placing your child in it. Avoid or remove any decorations or toys with small parts your child could swallow—in particular check stuffed animals and dolls for eyes, buttons, or other accoutrements that could be pulled off and ingested. If floor or table lamps are used, check that they are out of reach so children can't pull them over. And place nonslip pads under rugs or mats if they don't already have them so no one slips on the floor.

TOUCH OF WHIMSY
Fun, colorful accents in this tween room clearly convey a bird theme. A brightly painted birdhouse sits in the built-in bookshelf, while finials on the bedposts also incorporate the handpainted, fanciful structures.

AHOY, MATEY
(ABOVE) A slew of accessories—including a treasure map, a flying gull, a miniature ship's wheel, and a sailor's hat—perfectly capture a nautical theme.

PRETTY IN PINK (BELOW) A dainty white chandelier with tiny crystal accents and custom pink shades adds a feminine touch.

contact information

The Home Depot® offers many of the elements that go into making complete kids' rooms, including paint, flooring, lighting, storage solutions, and accessories. This extensive inventory offers customers a comprehensive and varied selection that will ensure your child's room truly reflects his or her personal style and taste while enabling you to stick to a realistic budget. Information on products and materials may be obtained from Home Depot stores or directly through manufacturers by mail, telephone, or online.

Contacting Meredith Corporation

To order this and other Meredith Corporation books, call 800/678-8091. For further information about the information contained in this book, please contact specific manufacturers and professionals or contact Meredith by e-mail at hi123@mdp.com or by phone at 800/678-2093.

Contacting The Home Depot®

For general information about product availability, contact your local Home Depot or visit The Home Depot® website at www.homedepot.com.

professionals

Listed are the names of and contact information for the professionals who worked on the new kids' rooms locations shot exclusively for The Home Depot® that are featured in this book.

8–11:
Field Editor—Sandra L. Mohlmann
Photographer—Josh Gibson
Interior Designer—Kim Dwyer, Lucy and Company, 1009 East Blvd., Charlotte, NC 28203; 704/342-6655

14–17, 161 (bottom), 167 (top right):
Field Editor—Sarah Needleman
Photographer—Jamie Hadley
Designer/mural artist—Lisa Konjicek-Segundo, Olive Juice Designs, 415/994-8747; www.olivejuicedesigns.com; lisa@olivejuicedesigns.com

20–23, 137 (bottom):
Field Editor—Sandra L. Mohlmann
Photographer—Josh Gibson
Faux artist—Keith Keim, Lucy and Company, 1009 East Blvd., Charlotte, NC 28203; 704/342-6655.
Interior Designer—Kim Dwyer, Lucy and Company, 1009 East Blvd., Charlotte, NC 28203; 704/342-6655.

36–37, 46–47, 128–129:
Field Editor—Diane Carroll
Photographer—Nancy Nolan
Architect—James Williams, AIA, Williams & Dean Associated Architects, Inc., 18 Corporate Hill Dr., Suite 210, Little Rock, AR 72205; 501/224-1900; www.williamsdean.com; jwilliams@williamsdean.com
Interior Designer—Robin Halbert-Petty, ASID, Williams & Dean Associated Architects, Inc., 18 Corporate Hill Dr., Suite 210, Little Rock, AR 72205; 501/224-1900; www.williamsdean.com

38–39, 116–117, 130–131:
Field Editor—Diane Carroll
Photographer—John Granen
Interior Designer—Abbey Francis, ASID, Sassy Sprouts; 314/520-6839; www.sassysprouts.com

40–43:
Field Editors—Erin Milgram & Sarah Needleman
Photographer—Jamie Hadley
Architect—Alan Levy (deceased)
Designer—City Studios, 2942 Turk Blvd., San Francisco, CA 94118; 415/386-2521; www.citystudiosinteriors.com
Contractor—W. John Build, 2736 Fulton St., San Francisco, CA 94118; 415/203-1107

44–45, 151 (top right), 156 (left middle):
Field Editor—Khristi Zimmeth

Photographer—Beth Singer
Decorative Painter/Designer—Jennifer Gushen Haver; 734/546-5830; www.jenniferhaver.com.

48–49:
Field Editor—Eileen A. Deymier
Photographer—Ross Chapple
Interior Designer—M. Kelley Astore, Wisteria & Roses, 11620 Cedar Chase Rd., Herndon, VA 20170; 703/421-3981

52–55, 148 (bottom):
Field Editor—Sandra L. Mohlmann
Photographer—Josh Gibson
Faux Artist—Keith Keim, Lucy and Company, 1009 East Blvd., Charlotte, NC 28203; 704/342-6655
Interior Designer—Beth Keim, Lucy and Company, 1009 East Blvd., Charlotte, NC 28203; 704/342-6655

62–65:
Field Editor—Sandra L. Mohlmann
Photographer—Josh Gibson
Interior Designer—Kim Dwyer, Lucy and Company; 1009 East Blvd., Charlotte, NC 28203; 704/342-6655

68–69:
Field Editor—Stacey Kunstel
Photographer—Sam Gray
Architects—William H. Soupcoff, AIA, & Shannon Alther, AIA, TMS Architects, 1 Cate St., Portsmouth, NH 03801;

603/436-4274; www.tmsarchitects.com
Builder/Contractor—Mark DePiero, DePiero Construction Management
Interior Designer—Michael Cebula, Cebula Design, Inc., 18 Liberty St., Newburyport, MA 01950; 978/462-6984

72–75, 120–121:
Field Editor—Diane Carroll
Photographer—Alise O'Brien
Interior Designer—Larry West, Interiors West, 400 N. Van Buren, Little Rock, AR 72205; 501/666-WEST (9378)

82–83:
Field Editors—Erin Milgram & Sarah Needleman
Photographer—Jamie Hadley
Designer—Daphne D. Light, Daphne D. Light Designs, 2440 Geary Blvd., Suite B, San Francisco, CA 94115; 415/860-0373; www.daphnedlightdesigns.com

86–89, 142 (bottom):
Field Editor—Diane Carroll
Photographer—Nancy Nolan
Interior Designer—Janna Toland, Cobblestone & Vine, 5100 Kavanaugh Blvd., Little Rock, AR 72207; 501/664-4988

90–91:
Field Editor—Diane Carroll
Photographer—John Granen
Interior Designer—Abbey Francis, ASID, Sassy Sprouts; 314/520-6839; www.sassysprouts.com
Painter—Vesper Studios, Fayetteville, Arkansas; 479/903-1659

index

a-b